How to Be IRISH

(even if you already are)

Sean Kelly
&
Rosemary Rogers

The authors wish to extend *buíochas* to...

Ron Barrett

Monie Begley

John Boswell

Patty Brown

Bob Downey

Bridie Duignan

Adrienne Goodman

The Irish Echo

Rosemary Kelly

Laoise MacReamoinn

Kathy McKeever

Nell Rogers Michlin

Eileen Murphy

Sally Ann O'Reilly

Beth Pearson

Kathleen Rogers

Oona Schmid

Barbara Schubeck

Shamrock Gift Shop

Ellen Wallop

and

Bruce Tracy

Copyright © 1999 by Sean Kelly and Rosemary Rogers

All rights reserved under International and Pan-American Copyright Conventions. Published in the United States by Villard Books, a division of Random House, Inc., New York, and simultaneously in Canada by Random House of Canada Limited, Toronto.

VILLARD BOOKS is a registered trademark of Random House, Inc.

Illustration credits begin on page 178.

Library of Congress Cataloging-in-Publication Data
Kelly, Sean.
How to be Irish (even if you already are) / Sean Kelly and Rosemary Rogers.
     p.   cm.
ISBN 0-375-75236-6
1. Irish Americans—Social life and customs—Humor. 2. Irish Americans—History—Humor. 3. Irish–Social life and customs—Humor. 4. Irish—History—Humor. I. Rogers, Rosemary. II. Title.
E184.I6K45 1999
973.049162—dc21   98–46156

Random House website address: www.atrandom.com

Printed in the United States of America on acid-free paper

98765432

First Edition

Design: Barbara Schubeck and Adrienne Goodman

For two of our favorite Irishmen,

Charles A. Kelly

and

Michael J. Rogers

LISTEN TO WHAT I'M TELLING YOU

The Ireland referred to throughout this text is
(except in Chapter 14) a wholly imaginary country, and the
word *Irish* (aka "the Sea-Divided Gael") designates an imaginary
race of humans descended from its original inhabitants.

For our purposes, the term is nonsectarian. The devout
Presbyterian whose clan has occupied County Down
for the past four hundred years has as good a claim to Irishness
as does any nonpracticing Catholic whose family has
been living in Chicago for the last century and a half.

HOW TO USE THIS BOOK

Throughout the text, helpful tips for faking typical Irish
attitudes, demeanor, and/or behavior—of the three possible
varieties—are indicated by means of the following symbols:
☙ Stage Irish   🎩 Lace-Curtain Irish   🐷 Shanty Irish.

When in doubt (as prior to any social engagement), simply
1) refer to the emergency by category—
eating, drinking, voting, sex, etc.,
2) consult therein your "sign," and
3) behave accordingly.

By the way, the epigraphs at the beginning of each
chapter are from James Joyce's *Ulysses*.

CONTENTS

John F. Kennedy

35th President of the United States

Born May 29, 1917
Entered Into Eternal Rest
November 22, 1963

THE WEARING OF
THE GREENING OF AMERICA

Sixteen percent of North Americans claim to be of Irish descent. And these days, the remaining 84 percent are green (mark you) with envy.

Because Irish is In.

Because everyone loves *Riverdance*. Because *Angela's Ashes* and *How the Irish Saved Civilization* topped the best-seller lists for years. Because Maeve Binchy and Roddy Doyle's hit novels become hit movies, and because *Titanic*, the hit movie of all time, contrasts the stultifying snobs in first class with the zesty Irish peasants below decks. Because everyone knows that Seamus Heaney is the world's greatest poet, Martin McDonagh is the world's greatest playwright, Joyce's *Ulysses* is the best novel of the century, U2 is the world's greatest rock band...

So Irish is In.

It was, of course, not always so. Like other immigrant groups since, the Irish in America were at first despised and excluded: "No Irish Need Apply," said the want ads. Next, their Irish-American children were patronized or marginalized. "What the hell do I have to do to be called an American?" demanded Joseph Kennedy. Finally, their grandchildren were nearly eliminated by assimilation. After JFK's election, the Irish very nearly (in the words of historian Noel Ignatiev) "became white."

But now, Irish is In.

Long-closeted Hiberno-Americans are coming proudly out, while preppies, yuppies, and other WASP trendies are ransacking their family trees, desperate to uncover a Mick in the woodpile of their roots. So to speak.

And so, for both the fallen-away Irish and for everyone else who longs to be—or to appear to be—just a wee bit Irish, we offer *How to Be Irish*.

CHAPTER 1

✿

TYPICAL IRISH (The Choice Is Yours)

—*We are all Irish, all king's sons.*
—*Alas, Stephen said.*

Various character flaws, ranging from simple incompetence to cold-blooded treachery, are dismissed by the Irish themselves as "typical Irish."

But you—in order to pass for "typical Irish"—must first decide what Irish "type" you wish to pass for. Your choices have been nicely spelled out for you in the opening pages of that classic of Irish-American literature, *Gone with the Wind*.

Stage Irish: Scarlett, we read, has "the easily stirred passions of her Irish father," Gerald O'Hara. A charming rogue, a natural-born rebel, and a drinking man, he is described as "florid" and "bandy-legged, short nosed, wide mouthed and belligerent…hard headed and blustering…the brogue heavy on his tongue…with a hair trigger of temper…with a loud bark but no bite at all." Gerald has gone so far as to name his plantation Tara, after the palace of the ancient high king of Ireland.

Lace-Curtain Irish: Gerald has scant use for the MacIntoshes, Tara's aristocratic (and possibly Abolitionist) neighbors, who are "Scotch-Irish and Orangemen from Ulster…close-mouthed and stiff necked…dour and independent."

Shanty Irish: The nearby tenant-farming Slatterys are dismissed even by the O'Hara's slaves as "white trash." He is "shiftless and whining," she "the snarly-haired mother to a brood of sullen and rabbity-looking children which increased every year."

So, sir or madam, which will it be for you? Stage, Lace-Curtain, or Shanty Irish?

♣

Now, it may be argued that surely there are other sorts of Irish. Unfortunately, this is not so, or is no longer so. Read on.

ANGLO-IRISH
(An Endangered Species)

Aka: the Ascendancy, the gentry, Old English, the *sassenach*, Sir John, West Britons.

Identifying characteristics: Georgian architecture, mildew, tweeds, high tea, high horses, high foreheads.

The first invaders from England to Ireland (in 1169) were not remotely "Anglo" anything. They spoke French, being descended from the Normans, who, exactly a century before, had invaded and occupied England itself. It was they who erected all those picturesque ruins—castles and round towers—with which the Irish landscape is yet graced.

Within a generation or two, these Butlers and de Burghs, FitzGeralds and Fitz-Maurices had gone native—become *Hibernis ipsis Hiberniores*, "more Irish than the Irish"—according to one distressed Saxon observer. They were Catholic, spoke only Gaelic, and drank to excess. For the ensuing five hundred years, they rebelled continuously against the Plantagenet/Lancaster/York/Tudor British Crown, invariably fought valiantly, and were invariably defeated. Thus, the Normans succeeded in becoming virtually Irish.

So, early in the seventeenth century, it was incumbent upon the Brits to introduce into Erin a new class of titled landlords—genuine Anglo-Saxons this time, and Protestants. On their behalf, most of the arable land was confiscated from the natives, the infamous Penal laws against the Catholics were enforced, and taxes, tithes, and "rack' rents" wrenched. These transplanted Puritans erected those other glories upon the Irish landscape, the "Great Houses," which are today, most of them, elegant, if moldy, B&Bs.

But—wouldn't you know it?—(alas for England!) it wasn't long before this "Protestant nation of Ireland" (as it was called by one of its leaders, Henry Flood) was itself transformed into a crowd of Irish "patriots." Irish independence—of one kind or another—was urged politically in parliament by Henry Grattan, savagely in print by Jonathan Swift, and fecklessly on the battlefield by Wolfe Tone and Robert Emmet—Protestants all. Exasperated with this disloyalty, Mother England responded, in 1801, with the Act of Union, which denied the separate existence of any such place as Ireland at all, at all.

Nevertheless, since then, many of the (Protestant) Anglo-Irish—most notably Charles Stuart Parnell ("Ireland's Uncrowned King"), the novelist Maria Edgeworth, the poet W. B. Yeats, and the playwright G. B. Shaw—continued to assert not only Ireland's unique identity, but their own identity as Irish.

In his 1989 *A Singular Country*, author J. P. Donleavy (American-born, and therefore something of a snob) assured us that "not all your living breathing ascendancy have disappeared," and implored us to "thank our lucky eccentric stars" that these "gentry folk are alive and kicking under their top hats and tiaras, and their smiles keep smiling from glossy social magazines."Well, maybe.

But for our purposes, such of the Anglo-Irish as now reside in the New World are, or might as well be, subset of the lace-Curtain Irish (See below).

BLACK IRISH
(A Tautology)

It is widely assumed that in their natural state the Irish are a chaste and cheerful, guileless, button-nosed people with freckles, smiling blue eyes, and red hair. Dark-haired, sexy, beaky, sneaky exceptions are known as Black Irish, whose existence is explained, in American folklore, by the prolific breeding habits of swarthy Iberian seamen who swam ashore to Ireland after the wreck of the Spanish Armada. Black Irish chaps not infrequently turn up as passionate, brooding, elusive love objects in mass-produced romance novels. Think Rhett Butler.

The awful truth is that all those archetypal Irish redheads are the genetic consequence of long-ago encounters between the damsels of Erin and lusty, red-headed Vikings. A series of annual Hiberno-Danish cross-breeding experiments commenced in 795, and continued for two centuries.

The Norsemen's mates—willing or otherwise—were Celts, a people who had themselves invaded Ireland only a few centuries before. And although some Celts seem to have been blonds—for which reason they were also known as Finns, that is, "fair-haired"—the aboriginal Irish, the rootstock of the place, were a Neolithic folk known (to the Celts) as Firbolgs, or Eirainn. They, like their cousins the Picts of Scotland, were a small, wiry, black-haired, dark-skinned people.

Arguing recently that "Ulster's problem is a racial one," psychologist Morris Fraser (*Children of Conflict*) has observed that, in Northern Ireland, "the Celtic group have darker hair and eyes, more swarthy complexions, and more angular features than their Anglo-Saxon counterparts."

BOG IRISH
(An Extinct Species)

Aka: conchies, crackers, croppies, hillbillies, rubes, pig-in-the-parlor Irish, plowboys.

Identifying characteristics: a spud, a pig, a well-tugged forelock, a pike, a shillelagh, a jug o' poteen.

Being originally from the countryside—the descendants of tenant farmers or dispossessed tenant farmers—they were less urban, and therefore less urbane, than even the city-slum-dwelling Shanty Irish. Thanks to two ice ages and a famously rainy climate, Ireland possesses large areas of wet, spongy soil, for which the very word, *bog*, is borrowed from the Gaelic. Upon these barren wastes (the only land not confiscated by their betters) the Gaelic-speaking paupers lived. From the bogs they harvested turf, or peat, which is rotted vegetable matter, including decomposed bog moss, aka sphagnum. Bricks of this stuff the Bog Irish dug up, stacked, and sundried, and then used to shingle their roofs and to burn as fuel.

The majority of nineteenth-century Irish immigrants to America had been, at home, such folk, "simple pea-sants...equipped with a knowledge of simple tillage, but having no money to secure the land or even to journey to the place where the land was." (*A History of American Life*, Arthur Schlesinger and Dixon Fox, eds.)

Denied access to New World bogs, many of these Irishmen and women settled in port-city slums, thereby becoming Shanty Irish. Eventually, a few of them—the least decent of them—evolved into Lace-Curtain Irish. (For these, gift-wrapped imported briquettes of bog peat are today available in New World, at about a buck a pound.)

LACE-CURTAIN IRISH
(A Flourishing Species)

Aka: the FIF (First Irish Families), IAPs (Irish-American Princes), HAPs (Hibernian-American Princesses), Castle Catholics, "cut-glass" Irish, "two-toilet" Irish.

Identifying characteristics: charity balls, money, power politics, grudges, tea breath, chronic constipation.

How to tell the Lace-Curtain Irish from the Shanty Irish: Shanty Irish are criminals and/or cops, but Lace-Curtain Irish are lawyers and/or judges; Shanty Irish are saloon keepers and/or drunks, but Lace-Curtain Irish are bootleggers who become distillers; Shanty Irish are ward heelers and/or agitators, but Lace-Curtain Irish are political officeholders and/or political pundits. Shanty Irish are priest-ridden; Lace-Curtain Irish call bishops by their first names. Lace-Curtain Irish have large families; the Shanty Irish breed like rabbits. Lace-Curtain Irish prefer the Latin mass, and deplore the Latino masses.

How to tell the Lace-Curtain Irish from the WASPS: Listen to what the WASPS say about them after they leave the room.

An entire book, *Real Lace* by Steven Birmingham, has been written about this class of Irish American, and so has a classic comic strip—George McManus's "Bringing Up Father," aka "Maggie and Jiggs."

Except on ceremonial occasions, e.g., election days, the Lace-Curtainers are in flight from, or denial of, their uncouth ethnicity. They believe that full acceptance into the American aristocracy may be achieved via a gentleman's B at an Ivy League (or Seven Sisters) college, followed by marriage to a Huguenot (or Episcopalian). The Kennedys manage this; the Buckleys do not—hence, "the Buckleys are only semi-semi-Irish, when compared with the Kennedys' full semi-Irishness." (Garry Wills, *The Kennedy Imprisonment*.)

Many Protestant American dynasties are Lace-Curtain Irish without knowing it, for the Great Crimes behind their Great Fortunes were committed by ancestors who were Scotch-Irish (See below).

A note on lace: in the Old Country, lace-making was a cottage industry, by which means poor convent girls and peasant women were able to earn a few pence. They or their families could not, of course, afford to buy their handiwork, which were exported to England. The Limerick Lace beloved of Lace-Curtain Irish-American tourists is—being machine-made and of cotton rather than linen—not "real lace" at all.

SCOTCH-IRISH
(A Semimythological Species)

Aka: fine old stock, good country people, Mr. Charlie, Orangemen, Prods, the silent majority, Scots-Irish.

Identifying characteristics: the stars and bars, the King James Bible, the first nickel they ever made, Skull and Bones, the GOP.

Celtic, but not Catholic, and therefore (almost) honorary Anglo-Saxons—a white race of hardworking, frugal, God-fearing, true-blue Southerners, dreamed up, in 1895, by American "historian" Samuel S. Green, who contended that America had been invented and settled by these descendants of Lowland Scottish Presbyterians. These Scotch-Irish had, allegedly, been transplanted in the seventeenth century (in a process begun by the British king James I and completed by the British dictator Oliver Cromwell) to "plantations" in the raped-and-pillaged (by the grace of God!) province of Ulster—whence they providentially departed for the "plantations" of the American South.

All rubbish, of course. While it is true that in the five years preceding the American Revolution 55,000 of such ambitious Protestant tradesfolk (victims of England's brutal new tariff policies, by the by) *did* emigrate to Dixie, they had been preceded thither by a quarter of a million Irish-Irish, who already composed one eighth of the South's entire white population.

Ethnologically, as well, the Scotch-Irish concept is specious: the west of Scotland—and Ulster—had always been a racially homogeneous, if migratory (Gaelic-speaking) society. In the sixth century, the native Scots were converted to Christianity by the Irish Saint Columcille; in medieval Latin, *Scotus* meant "Irish-born"; in the fourteenth century, Scotland's king Robert the Bruce was Irish chieftain Hugh O'Neill's son-in-law, and so on.

But no sooner had most historians ditched the Scotch-Irish concept than David Hackett Fischer published (in 1988) *Albion's Seed: Four British Folkways in North America*. In support of his thesis, he asserts that the thousands of eighteenth-century immigrants from Ireland, who called themselves Irish, and who were called Irish, were in fact "North Britons."

SHANTY IRISH
(A Numerous Species)

Aka: corner boys, dead end kids, the lumpen proletariat, rednecks, white trash.

Identifying characteristics: bricks, Danny Boy, shovels, rosaries, a litter of brats, eczema patches, nylon stockings rolled over the knee and tied in a knot, oatmeal stains

Even the word for the hovels in which they dwelled, once thought to be derived from the Gaelic for "old house"— *sean tig*—is now believed to be from the French for "log hut," *chantier*.

There is no need to describe here the pitiful tribulations of Old Country Bog Irish. With his parody *The Poor Mouth*, Flann

O'Brien may have put an end (please God!) to the the genre of suffering-rural-peasant Irish autobiography. But the genre of suffering-city-dwelling-peasant autobiography—invented by door-knocking O'Casey, maintained by Borstal boy Behan, and typed by means of Christy Brown's left foot—continues to thrive. *Angela's Ashes* is only the most recent—and best-selling—example.

Once in America, the Shanty Irish adapted with impressive skill to the role of an American underclass. The men—big strapping fellows—were lazy, but some of them showed a talent for professional sports or show business. The women were pretty enough in their way, but made terrible servants, and bred like rabbits. The young boys formed gangs with scary names, rendered the streets unsafe, and played loud music. Their political leaders were either bloodthirsty radicals or corrupt demagogues. The lot of them were superstitious, frequently under the influence of substances, and, in general, a drain on the economy.

In the fullness of time, the Shanty Irish have been obliged to surrender their underclass hegemony to other, more worthy, ethnic groups, and are now practically indistinguishable from *boobus Americanus*.

(One difference between Shanty and Lace-Curtain Irish is that in the homes of the latter, the prominently displayed photo of JFK is autographed.)

STAGE IRISH
(A Ubiquitous Species)

Aka: Professional Irish, Bridey, "Himself," "Herself," Mick, Paddy, Yer Man.

Identifying characteristics: a twinkle in one eye, a tear in the other, a glass raised on high, a nose like a strawberry, shamrocks galore.

It was Samuel Johnson who observed, "The Irish are a fair people. They never speak well of one another." And, since the nastiest thing the Irish can call one another is "Stage Irish," they do it all the time. It implies that the accused is not only a

sham and a bore, but also a racial embarrassment.

So, in one another's critical presence, the Irish have the choice of 1) disguising their Irishness, and thus acting "West British," or 2) flaunting it, and being Stage Irish. It's no wonder they drink.

The original Stage Irishman appeared (where else?) onstage: as the hot-tempered comic-relief Captain MacMorris, in Shakespeare's *Henry V*. "… my nation? What ish my nation? Who talks of my nation?… so Chrish save me, I will cut off your head."

For centuries since, the swaggering, blustering, brogue-talking Stage Irishman has been a stock character in English-language comic drama—the best of which (need we observe?) has always been written by Irishmen.

"Not only do 'stage' Irishmen abound to this day, but they are far pleasanter than the other kind," attests Honor Tracy in *Mind You, I've Said Nothing*, although, in his "Cruiksheen Lawn" column for the *Irish Times*, Flann O'Brien used to rail against "these bought-and-paid-for Paddys...putting up the witty celtic act, doing the erratic but loveable playboy, pretending to be morose and obsessed and thoughtful...lazy, boozy, impulsive, hospitable, decent and so on till you weaken."

The Stage Irish woman is a vivacious and radiant girl who can (and will) be transformed in an eye-twinkle into a sorrowing maternal crone. And vice versa. She is Yeats's beloved Maud Gonne as Cathleen ni Houlihan, or the image of Sir John Lavery's wife in the same role, as long featured on the Irish pound note. (Lady Lavery was, interestingly enough, an American.) She is mournful as Deirdre of the Sorrows. She is stubborn as Maureen O'Hara in *The Quiet Man*. She is naughty as Molly Bloom. She is feisty enough to rip up a picture of the pope on network TV. She is Mother Machree.

A THEATRICAL HISTORY OF STAGE IRISH

Teague
The Twin Rivals (1702)
by the Ulster-born George Farquhar

Captain O'Blunder
The Brave Irishman (1743)
by Dubliner Thomas Sheridan

Connolly
The School for Wives (1773)
by Hugh Kelly

Sir Lucius O'Trigger
The Rivals (1775)
by Richard Brinsley Sheridan

Pat Rooney
the mischievous houseboy in
The Power Omnibus, New York (1833)

Mose the Bow'ry B'hoy in
A Glance at New York (1848)

The Heroes of Dion Boucicault's
popular melodramas from
The Colleen Bawn (1869)
to *The Shaughraun* (1873)

Members of the Mulligan Guard
hit Broadway revues (1878–1901)
by Harrigan and Hart

The Countess Cathleen
The Countess Cathleen (1901)
by William Butler Yeats

Barney Doran
John Bull's Other Island (1904)
by George Bernard Shaw

Christy Mahon and Pegeen Mike
The Playboy of the Western World (1907)
by J. M. Synge

"Fluther" Good
The Plough and the Stars (1926)
by Sean O'Casey

Phil Hogan
A Moon for the Misbegotten (1943)
by Eugene O'Neill

Monsewer
The Hostage (1958)
by Brendan Behan

Johnnypateenmike
The Cripple of Inichmaan (1996)
by Martin McDonagh

HOW IRISH ARE YOU, ANYWAY?

Take this simple quiz and find out.

🍀 **Who complained about "loathsome Irish relations"?**

   a) Madonna's uncle, upon hearing of his niece's liaison with Rosie O'Donnell

   b) Adolf Hitler, when his sister-in-law, Brigid, and nephew, Patrick, visited Berlin

   c) Peter Lawford, once he got started on his ex-in-laws

answer: b

🍀 **"I'd advise you to go into hiding," was the warning issued by:**

   a) Dorothy Kilgallen's agent, after it was revealed that the gossip columnist could peek through her mask and see the "Mystery Guest" on *What's My Line*

   b) friends of the beloved Bishop Casey, when his illegitimate children showed up

   c) Samuel Beckett's publisher, when he wired the shy author that he had won the Nobel Prize

answer: c

🍀 **Shepherd Moons is:**

   a) an Irish variation of the dish shepherd's pie, featuring turnips

   b) the title of a best-selling Enya CD

   c) Aer Lingus code that author Maeve Binchy, who requires two seats, is coming aboard

answer: b

🍀 **Benwee Head is:**

   a) Garth Brooks's booking agent in Dublin

   b) a term of endearment applied to Regis Philbin in his days at Notre Dame

   c) a mountain in County Mayo

answer: c

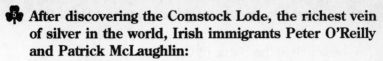

5 After discovering the Comstock Lode, the richest vein of silver in the world, Irish immigrants Peter O'Reilly and Patrick McLaughlin:

a) built Our Lady Queen of Martyrs, the largest Roman Catholic cathedral west of the Mississippi

b) died broke

c) returned to Ireland to help the orphans of the potato famine

answer: b

6 *Broim* signifies:

a) a small goatskin drum employed every August in the harvest dance of Lughnasa

b) the area of County Clare where the virginal Saint Dympna sought refuge from her incestuous father, king Damon

c) "fart" in Gaelic

answer: c

7 The average citizen of the Irish Republic annually eats how many pounds of potatoes?

a) 286

b) 65

c) 50

answer: a

8 "The love that dares not speak its name" refers to the relationship between:

a) an Irish priest and his housekeeper

b) Oscar Wilde and Lord Alfred Douglas

c) Bing Crosby and his pipe

answer: b

9 Dunbar Rover is:

a) a nightly news announcer on Radio Telefis Eireann

b) a member of a popular Gaelic football team

c) a type of potato

answer: c

🍀 **"You'll not take me!"** was the cry uttered by:

a) Grace O'Malley, the "Pirate Queen," when besieged at the Battle of Clew Bay

b) Irish immigrant "Typhoid Mary" Mallon, when confronted by U.S. health inspectors

c) Outlaw Ned Kelly, the "Wild Colonial Boy," when surrounded by the Australian police and shot twenty-two times

answer: c

🍀 **In his 1958 audience with Pope Pius XII, Frank Sinatra was tormented because:**

a) Il Papa kept grilling him about his Mafia connections

b) a Vatican monsignor asked him how long it had been since his last confession

c) the audience consisted of papal gushing about Bing Crosby's rapturous rendition of "Adeste Fideles"

answer: c

🍀 **Emma Whelan, a native of County Cork, snuck candy out of her young son's Christmas stocking. The lad blamed his lifelong food obsession on this incident and blew up to be:**

a) Boy George

b) Alfred Hitchcock

c) Diamond Jim Brady

answer: b

Two bonus rhetorical questions:

♣ Forbidden to own property, to practice their ancient religion, or to speak their ancient language, as paupers they made their way from Europe to the New World, where they inhabited crowded city tenements. At first mocked and despised, their descendants have become the most financially successful and best-educated of all "ethnic" groups. Are they:

a) the Irish?
b) the Jews?

♣ This island nation (a former British colony) is slowly recovering from centuries of economic hardship, partly as a result of its booming tourist industry; it is world famous for its hospitable natives and glorious scenery. Its exports to America however, are limited to strong liquor, pop musicians, and nannies. Is it:

a) Ireland?
b) Jamaica?

CHAPTER 2

✾

HOW TO HAVE AN IRISH NAME

—The mockery of it, he said gaily.
Your absurd name…My name is absurd too.

SURNAMES: BEYOND O' AND MAC

If your last name—or the surname of one of your forbears—begins with an *O'*, *Mac*, *Mc*, or *Fitz*, no one can question your right to claim that you're Irish.

There is, incidentally, nothing to the notion that *Mc* is Irish and *Mac* is Scottish. *Mac* means "son of" in Gaelic, the language of both the Scots and Irish, and it was sometimes written down (time being of the essence) by means of the abbreviation *Mc*. An *O'* means "descended from" or "of the family of," and suggests that your parents may not have amounted to much, but *their* ancestors were somehow special. *Fitz* (from the French *fils*, meaning "son") is Norman-Irish.

Murphy, Kelly, and Sullivan, are, in that order, the most common Irish family names in both Ireland and North America. They can be, and sometimes are, tarted up as McMurphy, O'Kelly, and O'Sullivan.

Naturally, all the old surnames had meanings in Gaelic: Sullivan means "one-eyed," Casey means "watchful," Daly signifies an "assemblyman," both Dunn and Donahue mean "swarthy," Kelly means either "contentious" or "sacred prostitute," and Kennedy translates as "ugly head."

Proud though their bearers may be, some common Irish family names are less than euphonious, and/or have unfortunate connotations in English. Consider: Boyle, Coote, Crampsy, Doody, Dooley, Flemming, Henn, Hickey, Hiney, Hog, Hoey, Hore, Looney, Meany, Morony, Moody, Mooney, Patchy, Roche, and Scully.

Although the phone books of Ireland contain plenty of O's and Mc's, they also list any number of such genuine Irish surnames as Adams, Bergen, Black(e), Brown(e), Butler, Carpenter, Carroll, Coffee, Cook(e), Ford, Fox, Green(e), Grimes, Kline, Lane, Lee, Leonard, Lewis, Robinson, Rogers, and, of course, Smith. This is because King Edward IV, in 1465, decreed that his Irish subjects must assume English translations of their Gaelic names.

Today, all Carpenters are entitled to resume being MacIntyres; Carters can go back to being McCarthys; Ryders, O'Marchachans; Stones, O'Mulclohys; and the Smiths can be McGowans once again.

TAKE BACK YOUR IRISH FAMILY NAME

English	Irish
Abbot	Aboid
Adams	Eadie
Black	Duff
Brown	Dunn
Clark	O'Cleirigh
Davis	McDaid
Johnson	MacShane
Jones	MacSeoin
Lee	Laoidhigh
Martin	MacMartain
Rogers	MacRuari
Taylor	Tailliuir
Thompson	MacThomais
Walsh	Brannagh
White	O'Galligan
Woods	Quill
Wright	Kicart
Young	Og

CHRISTIAN NAMES:
BEYOND KEVIN AND SHEILA

Increasingly popular given names in America are Kelly, Tara, Tyrone, and Shannon. But why name your kids after a color, a mound, a county, or an airport?

Instead, give the boys *real* Irish names, like Alphonsus, Finbar, Declan, or Fergus. Attracta, Dympna, or Fionualla will do nicely for the girls. But beware of calling a daughter Mary—some of  the native Irish, in their devotion to the Mother of God, consider the indiscriminate use of Her Holy Name to be blasphemous, and when christening their daughters resort to variations on it, e.g., Maire, Muire, Maura, and Maureen. Any of these names assures that the life of the bearer will be a vale of tears.

The venerable Irish Christian names Kevin and Sheila (the former honoring a misogynist hermit, the latter meaning a female of the fairy class) have long been adopted by other tribes.

At home and abroad, the most politically correct Irish often take to "Irishizing" the English-looking names that their careless parents applied to them. The tradition may have begun with patriot-martyrs Edmund Kent and Sean MacDermott, who signed Ireland's 1916 Declaration of Independence (and their own death warrants) as Eamon Ceannt and Sean Mac Diarmada. Dublin playwright John Casey took

Sean O'Casey as his *nom de plume*, and novelists John Whelan and Liam O'Flaherty turned into Sean O'Faolain and Liam O Flaitheartaigh. Kellys have been reborn as O Ceallaighs, O'Sullivans as O Suilleabhains, and Murphys as O Murchadhas. Even Kevin and Sheila may regain their ethnic purity when spelled Caoimhin and Sile.

In order to pass for Irish, it is quite permissible to rename yourself. For reasons best known to themselves, Irish men and women are seldom called by their real, that is, baptismal first names, anyway—e.g., Harry "Bing" Crosby, Francis "F. Scott" Fitzgerald, William "Jack" Dempsey, Herbert "Jackie" Gleason, Paul "Bono" Hewson, William "Ben" Hogan, Daniel "Pat" Moynihan, Mary "Flannery" O'Connor, Thomas "Tip" O'Neill, Peter "Fulton" Sheen, and so on.

But be advised, the inevitable abbreviation or variation of your first name is a surefire indicator of the type of Irish you are—or wish to pass for.

Name	*Stage*	*Lace-curtain*	*Shanty*
Ann	Annie	Anne	Nan
Brian	Brendan	Brandon	Bren
Bridget	Biddy	Bride	Bridey
Charles	Cormac	Chuck	Charlie
Daniel	Danny	Dan	Dinny, Dinty
Edward	Eammon	Teddy, Ed	Eddie
Eugene	Egan	Owen	Gene
Frances	Fanny	Frannie	Frankie
Francis	Frank	F.X.	Frankie
Helen	Eileen	Eleanor	Nellie
James	Seamus	Jim	Jake, Jimmy
Joan	Siobhan	Jo, Joanne	Joanie
John	Sean	Jack	Johnny
Kathleen	Kitty	Kay, Kick	Kate, Katie
Margaret	Pegeen, Peggy	Meagan, Meg	Maggie
Mary	Maureen	Marie	Mo
Michael	Mick, Mickey	Mitchell	Mike
Patricia	Patsy	Pat, Trisha	Patty
Patrick	Paddy, Pat	P.J.	Packy
Roger	Rory	Roderick	Roddy
Rosemary	Rosie	Rosemarie	Ro
William	Liam	Bill	Willie

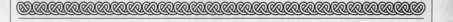

A MICK IN THE WOOD PILE?

Stokely Carmichael

Kathleen Cleaver

Edward Kennedy "Duke" Ellington

Ella Fitzgerald

Tommy Flanagan

Curt Flood

Dizzy Gillespie

Carl "The Mailman" Malone

Hattie McDaniel

Butterfly McQueen

Eddie Murphy

Toni Morrison

Chico O'Farrill

Shaquille O'Neal

Ron "Superfly" O'Neal

Chris Rock

CHAPTER 3

HOW TO TALK IRISH

—I'm ashamed I don't speak the language myself.
I'm told it's a grand language by them that knows.

THE AULD TONGUE

When passing for Irish, it is not necessary to speak Irish (Yeats couldn't), but it is essential to be passionately in favor of its preservation (Yeats was).

The Irish language (called *Gaelige*, and also known, unfortunately, as Erse) is a variety of Gaelic, the tongue of the ancient Celts. *Gaelige* was first banned in 1366, by the Statute of Kilkenny (a document written in French), but it survived 750 years of systematic suppression by the English. It only began to die in 1925, when the Irish government made it compulsory.

Clearly, the rules for transposing spoken Gaelic into the Roman alphabet were drawn up by a committee of men who were not only drunk, but *mean* drunk.

So, they decided that *mh* is pronounced "v" before a vowel, otherwise "w"...but *ui* is also "w." They never employed a single vowel when a diphthong would do—thus "a" is (sometimes) spelled *aoi*. Lower case *n* and *g* appear at random in front of words, but are never pronounced. A *d* or a *gh* may, apparently, be dropped at any point into any word—and they are not pronounced, either.

Seanbhean, which means old woman, is not pronounced "seen-been," but "shan-van"—because the Gaelic *s* is soft, *ea* is pronounced "ah" (unless there is an accent over the *a*, in which case it is "aw"), and "v" is also spelled *bh*.

The "f" sound may be indicated by *f, hf, p,* or *ph*. (So the name Francis is written *Proinsias*, but telephone is *teileafon*, and *raidhfil* is pronounced "rifle"—which it means).

In the 1930s, the Emerald Isle was adorned with billboards

urging the populace to learn and speak Gaelic. They were all, of course, in English.

In Ireland today, written Gaelic still appears only on road signs, to impress and/or confuse the tourists.

! ! ! ! ! *A Naisiun* Once Again ! ! ! ! !

A revival of the Irish language has been understood to be a prerequisite for Irish political independence ever since Young Irelander Thomas Davis declared in 1843 that "Only by baptism at the font of Gaelicism will we get the strength and ardor to fit us for freedom."

Padraic Pearse, leader of the 1916 rising, prophesied a future Ireland "not free merely but Gaelic as well, not Gaelic merely but free as well."

In the opinion of Michael Collins, who won the war against England in 1922, "Until we have [our language] again on our tongues and in our minds, we are not free."

In his 1943 address to the nation, De Valera warned that "With the language gone we could never aspire again to being more than half a nation."

Doubtless, all these statesmen had in mind the example of the United States of America, which had thrown off the yoke of British tyranny only after obliging all its citizens to converse in indigenous Algonkian.

A LITTLE IRISH DICTIONARY
or A Leprechaun's Lexicon

The Irish have contributed thousands of books, and even a few actual *words* to the English language: perhaps you've been speaking Irish all your life, without knowing it.

ballyhoo: a carnival barker's flamboyant "come-on"; hence, advertising and publicity in general. It is derived, it would seem, from the name of the Irish town of Ballyhooly—but nobody knows why.

bard: a poet. The bardoi were the highly regarded (and feared) minstrels of the Celts, tribal historians as well as court entertainers. Shakespeare, "the Bard of Avon," was probably *not* of Irish descent, despite the desperate efforts of Eugene O'Neill's father and William Butler Yeats to prove that he was.

barney: 1. a spree; 2. a rustic, clod

dish fellow; 3. a fixed prizefight, horse race, or other sporting event. Barney is the name of a castle in Ulster.

biddy: 1. a chick or hen, from the Gaelic *bideach*, meaning very small; 2. a female servant; 3. an elderly, gossipy woman. Both 2 and 3 are derived from the common diminutive of the Irish name Bridget.

blarney: 1. smooth, flattering talk; nonsense; lies. In 1602, Cormac McCarthy was supposed to surrender Blarney Castle to the surrounding English forces, but delayed doing so by means of delivering "soft speeches" until his conqueror, Lord President Carew, became a London laughingstock, "the dupe of the lord of Blarney." 2. in U.S. criminal slang, a lock picker.

bog: soggy, waterlogged ground. The Gaelic word for soft is *bog*.

boycott: a protest by means of economic coercion. In 1880, the Irish Land League declared a "rent strike" against Captain Charles C. Boycott, who was the land agent for a county Mayo landlord, the earl of Erne, master of Lough Mask House.

brannigan: a drinking bout, a spree; from the Irish family name.

brat: an unruly child. The Old Gaelic word *brat* signified cloth—hence (?) a diaper.

brogue: English as spoken ("mispronounced") with an Irish accent; an allusion to quaint Irish attire—in Gaelic a *bróig* is a shoe.

burke: to murder by suffocation, hence to suppress (an inquiry). Honoring William Burke, Irish-born murderer and supplier of cadavers to the Edinburgh School of Medicine, circa 1820.

car: a wheeled vehicle. From the Irish *carr*, the term for the war chariots of the Celts, according to Julius Caesar.

cracker: 1. a "poor white" of the American South, especially a native of Georgia; 2. "a noisy, boastful fellow" (Johnson's *Dictionary*). In Gaelic *craic* means pleasant talk, witty conversation. (This sense survives in the expression *wisecrack*.)

donovan: British slang; a potato. From the common Irish surname.

Donnelly: a strong blow with the fist. Honoring Irish prizefighter Daniel Donnelly, 1788–1820.

donniker: 1. (U.S. slang) a latrine, a filthy place; 2. the buttocks; 3. the penis; 4. a railway brakeman. From the common Irish surname Donegan.

donnybrook: a brawl, a riot, a free-for-all. The rowdiness of Donnybrook Fair, at one time an annual (August) event in a town near Dublin, was legendary.

dooley: railroad workers' slang for dynamite; from the Irish family name. (In America, Irish immigrants often worked in railway construction.)

galore: in abundance. From the Gaelic *go leor*, a sufficiency.

grogans: "muttonchop" side whiskers, presumably in the style once sported by an anonymous Irishman of that name.

hoodlum: from Muldoon, the name of an Irish gang leader in San Francisco, circa 1870; back-slang, with—presumably—a typo.

hooligan: a violent young criminal. The Houlihans were a large, spirited Irish family in Southwark, London, circa 1900. Hooligan has become the official Russian term for ruffian; whence—

Hooligan navy: the U.S. Coast Guard.

hoolihan: cowboy slang for "bulldogging" a steer to the ground. From the Irish surname Houlihan.

hubbub: a commotion. Derived from the ancient Irish war cry *abu!*

keen: a loud wail. In Irish *caoiane* is the term given to a weeping lamentation, a funeral song. At one time, professional "keeners" were hired to perform at Irish wakes.

kelly: 1. a shade of green; 2. a derby hat; 3. the game of rotation pool also known as "eight ball"; 4. the topsoil that is removed in order to get at the clay for making bricks. (The Irish were often employed in the construction industry, as hod carriers and bricklayers.)

kelt: African-American slang term for white woman, or light-skinned black woman. From *Celt*, i.e., Irish.

kibosh: to veto, squelch, put an end to. Not, as widely assumed, a Yiddishism, but from the Gaelic *cie bais*, "the cap of death."

limerick: a five-line verse, almost invariably obscene. Its connection to the Irish county and city of the same name is obscure.

lynch law: mob law, followed by swift execution. James Lynch, a fifteenth-century mayor of Galway, hanged his own son.

malarkey: excessive flattery, hot air. Possibly in honor of Malachy, an Irish saint to whom a series of baroque prophesies are (falsely) attributed.

McCarthyism: political witch-hunting. The clan name of U.S. senator Joseph McCarthy (1909–57) is derived from the Gaelic *cartach*, which means "loving."

McCoy: in U.S. slang, "the real McCoy" signifies "the genuine article." The phrase does not, contrary to popular opinion, honor the celebrated prizefighter "Kid" McCoy—whose real name was Norman Selby, anyway—but rather a prohibition-era bootlegger, William McCoy, whose merchandise was first-rate.

mickey: 1. high-spirited arrogance, a characteristic attributed to bearers of the common Irish Christian name of Michael; 2. the penis—Molly Bloom, in Joyce's *Ulysses*, employs *mickey* to signify the male organ of generation; 3. a roasted potato; 4. a small bottle of liquor; 5. an inmate of a penal institution.

mickey finn: a drugged drink, usually containing chloral hydrate, as first served by a nineteenth-century Irish-American bartender by that name, in Chicago's Lone Star Saloon.

mulligan: 1. in golf, an (illegal) second drive off the tee; 2. in hobo slang, a watery beef stew. In either case, it seems to have been named for a once-popular pepper sauce served in Irish-American saloons.

murphy: U.S. slang; 1. a potato, from the common Irish family name (which in Gaelic means "sea warrior")—hence, *murphy trap* means "mouth"; in lunch-counter slang, *Noah's boy and murphy* means "ham and potatoes"; 2. a police officer; 3. a swindle.

murphy bed: a foldaway bed, invented by William L. Murphy, died 1959.

murphy game: American; a confidence trick, a swindle (See *phoney*).

murphy money: baseball slang—a *per diem*, meal money.

murphy's countenance: a pig's head, British usage, circa 1810.

noggin: a container, hence (in slang) the head. From the Irish word *nogin*, meaning a wooden cup.

John O'Brien: U.S. hobo slang; a boxcar.

paddy: 1. an Irishman; 2. a gristle of roast meat. It is the customary diminutive of the common Irish Christian name Padraig. The Irish-crewed fishing cutters in nineteenth-century Boston Harbor were known as "paddy boats."

paddy wagon: a police van—often driven by Irishmen, presumably with cargoes of same.

paddywhack: 1. an Irishman; 2. a fit of temper.

phoney: fraudulent, counterfeit. In Gaelic, *fáinne* (pronounced "fawny"), means "a ring". "Fawny-dropping" was a confidence game practiced in the streets of eighteenth-century London.

quiz: a word of mysterious origin, but allegedly invented on a bet, circa 1780, by a Dublin theater manager named Thomas Daly.

shamus: hard-boiled slang for a detective or a private eye. In all likelihood derived from the common Irish name Seamus—and yet it has been proposed, in all seriousness, that the word is derived from the

Yiddish *shammes*, the ninth candle on a hanukkah menorah.

shanty: a shack or hovel. Possibly from the Gaelic *sean tig*, meaning "old house."

shebeen: an illegal drinking establishment; whence the American slang term "the whole shebang." Irish *seibin*, a little mug.

shenanigans: foolishness, horseplay. The Irish word for loitering is *sionnachuighim*.

slob: from the Irish word for mud, *slab*.

slogan: an identifying motto, or advertising tag line. Derived from the Gaelic *slaughghaim*, a war cry.

smithereens: tiny fragments, as in "blown to smithereens." Directly from the Gaelic *smidireens*.

tits: the female breasts. The Old English word "tits" was supplanted, after 1066, by the French *teats*, and disappeared entirely from use. The Gaelic word *diddies*, however, was transported to the American South where, transformed by Black English, it became *titties*, and, finally, *tits* again. Curiously, another American slang term for breasts is *murphies*.

Tory: a political conservative. From the Gaelic *toraidhe*, a criminal, a fugitive, a thief.

whiskey, whisky: alcoholic liquor distilled from grain. The Gaelic word for water is *uisce*.

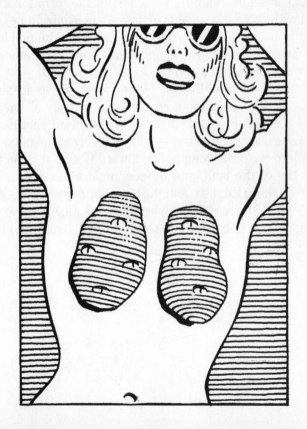

THE BROGUE

When you board an Aer Lingus flight to Ireland, you'll be greeted by flight attendants speaking in mellifluous, cultured tones—with just a trace of what might be described as "friendly British." This is the accent of rarefied upper-middle-class Dublin. You probably won't hear it again—unless you're a Joyce scholar on your way to a seminar—until it's time to confirm your return flight.

Now, a Scottish dialect is called a "burr," in recognition of the Scots Gaelic–speaker's trilled and guttural pronunciation of *r*. And all twenty-two of the distinct dialects spoken in England—Cockney, Yorkshire, etc.—are named in honor of the geographical areas in which they occur. But the term for English spoken with an Irish accent is *brogue*—a patronizing pejorative derived from the Celtic word for "a peasant's untanned leather shoe." Because, to refined English ears, the Irish sound as if they have shoes in their mouths.

"It hath ever been the use of the conqueror to despise the language of the conquered, and to force him by all means to learn his," wrote England's beloved Elizabethan poet Edmund (*The Faerie Queene*) Spenser—putting nicely at the outset England's three-centuries-long policy toward Gaelic and the Gaels. By the law of the land, and by economic necessity, the Irish started speaking English, and the word for the resulting dialect is first recorded circa 1700—when *brogue*'s meanings were (as you might expect) both Irish-inflected English and...a cheat.

There are three elements to a brogue, or any other dialect: vocabulary, pronunciation, and grammar. (Pay attention now!)

1. Vocabulary. Those wishing to pass for Irish are advised to "salt" their speech with the odd Gaelic word.

♕ Lace-Curtain Irish are advised to utter the Gaelic toast *slainte* when raising a (Waterford crystal–filled) glass (of Black Bush).

☙ Practitioners of Stage Irish must refer to all females as colleens, and occasionally ejaculate the dog-Irish phrase "Erin go Bragh!"

🐷 Shanty Irish may, and will, refer to their neighbors as *gobshites*.

2. Pronunciation. Many non-Anglophones have trouble with the English *th* sound. The French and Germans make it come out *z*, but Gaelic speakers say *d*—or, in the Irish Midlands, *t*. Thus, the Irish pronounce (and spell) the name Patrick as "Padraig." So, "Lilli Bulero," an enormously popular anti-Jacobin ballad (circa 1687), comically mocked a defeated "Jacobite" Irish patriot's saying "de" for *the* and "dat" for *that*. In the west, an s preceding a consonant is "soft." Thus *stop* becomes "shtop," and *stick* is a "shtick."

🐷 Luckily for them, most people who are, or wish to be taken for, Shanty Irish *already* say "dis, dat, dese, and dose," and, having a drop taken, slur their *s*'s.

Many of the native Irish first learned to speak English early in the eighteenth century, and they still pronounce certain words as their overlords did back then. In Dublin today, as in the poems of Alexander Pope, *tea* is pronounced to rhyme with day.

☙ This being the case, speakers of Stage Irish are advised to employ the *d/th* transposition and to muck about shamelessly with vowels, as in: "Oi" for *I*, "niver" for *never*, "slaype" for *sleep*, "wid" for *with*, "mee" for *my*, "woif" for *wife*.

♕ Lace-Curtain Irish, who attend fine prep schools precisely in order to shed their "accents," must fall back on Anglo-Irish, e.g., "shed-yule" for *schedule*, "chewsday" for *Tuesday*, etc.

3. Grammar. Gaelic is more than somewhat peculiar—for example, its verbs have no infinitive form. So anyone thinking in Irish but talking in English will say "It's sorry you'll be" instead of "You're going to be sorry." And since the language lacks the verb "to have," the pluperfect tense ("I had gone") becomes "I was after going."

In order to pass for Irish, read and reread *Riders to the Sea*. It'll soon have you crooning lovely, lilting things like "T'was murmur we did for a gallus potion would rouse a friar, I'm thinking, and he limp with leching." And never you mind that isn't Synge, but Joyce mocking him.

But all of this is…academic. When passing for Irish, there is no need to affect a brogue, authentic or otherwise, until everyone's been so over-served that no one will remember a word you utter.

WHEN YOU WISH UPON A STAR

American movie actors have frequently been called upon to attempt brogues, with decidedly mixed results.

SOME GOOD EXAMPLES:

Ned Beatty, as the elusive tenor Josef Locke in *Hear My Song*, 1991.

Marlon Brando, arbitrarily disguised as an old biddy and doing a flawless imitation of Richard Harris's Limerick accent in *The Missouri Breaks*, 1976. (This was payback time—Harris had given Brando a nasty bop on the nose on the set of *Mutiny on the Bounty*).

Richard Kiley, very effective as Diane Keaton's clueless father in *Looking for Mr. Goodbar*, 1977.

Thomas Mitchell, as Scarlett's blustering dad in *Gone With the Wind*, 1939.

Robert Mitchum, catching the lilt while eschewing the accent in *Ryan's Daughter*, 1970.

Brad Pitt, who manages an Ulster accent in *The Devil's Own*, 1997.

Mickey Rourke, as a hit man with the same difficult accent, in *A Prayer for the Dying*, 1987.

Orson Welles, as Rita Hayworth's admirer in *Lady from Shanghai*, 1948.

OTHERWISE:

Fred Astaire, not half trying in *Finian's Rainbow*, 1968.

Humphrey Bogart, half trying as Michael O'Leary in *Dark Victory*, 1939

Tom Cruise and **Nicole Kidman**, trying very hard in *Far and Away*, 1992.

Julia Roberts, when it occurred to her, in *Mary Reilly*, 1996 and *Michael Collins*, 1996.

Barbara Stanwyck, most amusingly, in *Union Pacific*, 1939.

BULLS

"'If the patients were deprived of tobacco,' reported Dr Myles to the committee of the Ballinasloe Lunatic Asylum, 'they would go mad,'"(*Pall Mall Gazette*, May 17, 1918).

When passing for Irish, you will be required to spice up your conversation by uttering the odd, amusing "bull." A bull is a blunder in speech, usually an inadvertent contradiction in terms, and is proverbially "Irish." The word itself may be derived from the Middle English *bul*, meaning a falsehood, or from the name of one Obadiah Bull, an Irish lawyer in the court of Henry VII. Or it may be a jesting reference to papal bulls, in which the pope assumes total authority while styling himself "servant of servants." Or perhaps it is just short for "a cock and bull story."

"Nobody goes there anymore—it's too crowded," is a brilliant example of a bull, attributed to the greatest living exponent of the form, baseball's great Yogi Berra—who is, unfortunately, not Irish.

"The profligacy of the age is such that we see little children not able to walk or talk running about the streets and cursing their maker," declared the past master of bulls, a reactionary Irish baronet named Sir Boyle Roche. He kept Parliament in stitches throughout the 1790s with his demands to know "what posterity has done for us," and assertions that "the country is overrun with absentee landlords."

It is said that if you see three cows lying down in a field, the one standing up is an Irish bull. Furthermore, as John Pentland Mahaffy, provost of Trinity College and legendary Dublin wit, observed, "an Irish bull is always pregnant."

It has been suggested that the Irish began to make bulls after being forced to join the Volunteers.

BLARNEY

The essential aspect of Irish speech is its content—that is to say, its total *lack* of content—that is to say, "blarney." Oscar Wilde is alleged, by James Joyce, to have said to William Butler Yeats—or is it the other way around?— "We Irish have done nothing, but we are the greatest talkers since the Greeks."

FDR is supposed to have asked Al Smith, "Why do you Irish always answer a question with a question?" To which the Happy Warrior replied, "Do we, now?"

It may be that the Gael's traditional long-winded response to a simple question results from the fact that the Gaelic language does not *have* words for *yes* or *no*.

KISS MY BLARNEYSTONE

An expedition is undertaken by many visitors to Ireland to the ruins of Blarney Castle, County Cork. There they assume a most uncomfortable and abject position and devoutly press their lips to a rock— preferably while being photographed—in the belief that they will thereby be granted the gift of eloquence. This deed accomplished, they are free to continue their journeys, snickering at all the outmoded Christian customs of the natives.

Over the bitter centuries, their own language stolen from them, the Irish acquired the gift o' the gab. They learned to lie to themselves, in order to make their lives bearable, and to lie to the English, on principle. In self-defense, they became a nation of storytellers and gobshites, poets and blather-skites, orators and flannelmouths. Blarney is not meant by its speaker to convey the truth; so if you believe it, it's your misfortune.

AER LINGUISTICS:
Contemporary Anglo-Hibernian

Astonish your friends and confound your enemies by the occasional use of guaranteed 100 percent contemporary Irish slang!

a drop, a glass, a spot, a touch: a drink (and not a small one).

amaddon: a fool (sometimes *cod* or *wanker*, never *eejit*).

amn't I?: aren't I? (a leftover eighteenth-century Anglicism).

aul' doll: wife (sometimes "the moth," but *never* "herself").

aul' fella: husband (not "himself").

bazz: pubic hair.

bazzer: a haircut.

blow: treat ("I'm blowing for dinner"). (See also *stand*.)

bollix: a mess, utter confusion; also the negative answer to a request.

bowsie: troublemaker.

brilliant: acceptable, okay, fine (has replaced *grand*).

crack: fun (from the Gaelic *craic*).

dead man: an empty glass, a collector of life insurance premiums.

dropsy: a tip.

evening: afternoon.

feck: *fuck*, as pronounced in the presence of a priest or female. (See *shite*.)

flah: a sexy woman.

flash: sexual intercourse.

flash bag: a woman of easy virtue.

foxer: a moonlighting job.

gobshite: a talkative, boring moron.

hoor: man, guy. (A pub greeting: "How're you hoors?")

I haven't a clue: don't ask me. (Has largely replaced "there you have me.")

Is the tea wet yet?: Is the tea ready?

jack: an erection.

jackeen: someone from Dublin; a city slicker.

langer: the penis, or a dislikable man.

mauser: a large woman.

maggot: unpleasant fellow.

mollycoddle: a mama's boy.

napper: the head, the brain.

neck: nerve, cheek, chutzpah.

nerves: mental illness.

not 100 percent: a total bollix (a rare example of Irish understatement).

of low stature: short (a rare example of Irish political correctness).

on the tablets: taking antidepressants and/or tranquilizers (a not-so-rare habit).

over the moon: moderately happy (has also replaced *grand*).

pissing: raining. Also *flaking, lashing*.

pooley: urine.

poxy: unpleasant, gross (but *poxed* means "very lucky").

queerhawk: a weirdo.

rainy day: moldy day, dirty auld day. It's raining: It's pissing, lashing, flaking.

a ride: a hunk, a babe, an attractive person of the opposite sex.

sheela: a man who takes inordinate interest in women's affairs—not a steamer, but possibly a mollycoddle.

shite: euphemism for *shit*.

shook: sick, old (*got shook* means "got old," *got horrid shook* means "got really old").

slag: run down, criticize.

stand: treat to a drink. ("Let me stand you a spot.")

The three classes may be distinguished by their uses of these common idiomatic expressions:

- Stage Irish: "Faith and Begorrah!" or alternately, "Shure and Begorrah!"
- Lace-Curtain Irish: "Oh, I say, raw-ther!"
- Shanty Irish: "Jesus, Mary, and Joseph!"

- Stage Irish: "Top o' the Morning."
- Lace-Curtain Irish: "Howdja do?"
- Shanty Irish: "G'day."

- Stage Irish: "Saints preserve us!"
- Lace-Curtain Irish: "Quelle dommage!"
- Shanty Irish: "Fecking hell!"

- Stage Irish: "Me sainted mither."
- Lace-Curtain Irish: "My late mater."
- Shanty Irish: "Ma, Lord have mercy on her soul."

- Stage Irish: "I had more than a passing acquaintance with John Barleycorn last night."
- Lace-Curtain Irish: "I'm a tad under the weather."
- Shanty Irish: "I'm gonna puke."

- Stage Irish: "She's in the family way."
- Lace-Curtain Irish: "She's studying abroad for a year."
- Shanty Irish: "She's up the pole."

THE JOYS OF IRISH

At the end of the twentieth century, Yiddish has worked its way into the American vernacular, tripping lightly off Gentile tongues. Can we not hope the same for Irish, another expressive, ethnic language that sounds suspiciously like Yiddish? Allegedly, Irish-American actor James Cagney would effortlessly slip from English to Yiddish to Irish and back again in the course of one conversation. And he was Yankee Doodle Dandy!

THEY SOUND ALIKE, BUT WATCH IT!

IRISH	YIDDISH
crappallach (restriction)	*kreplach* (dumpling)
fagalach (laggard)	*fagallah* (male homosexual)
puth (scent)	*putz* (penis)
scliep (gaiety)	*schlep* (drudge)
speal (scythe)	*schpiel* (sales pitch)
naofa (holy)	*nafka* (streetwalker)
bubanach (bubonic plague)	*bubala* (darling one)

THEY SOUND ALIKE AND MEAN THE SAME!

ENGLISH	IRISH	YIDDISH
smear	*smear*	*schmear*
buxom	*sodog*	*zaftig*
thief	*gadai*	*gonif*
penis	*slat*	*schmuck*
foreigner	*gall*	*goy*
troubles	*triobloid*	*tsouris*
stupid person	*duraman*	*dumkopf*
excrement	*cac*	*drek*

USE INTERCHANGEABLY!

ENGLISH	IRISH	YIDDISH
face	*eadan*	*punum*
drunkard	*meisceoir*	*schicker*
busy body	*bumbog*	*yenta*
agitated	*oibrithe*	*farmisht*
complainer	*easaoid*	*kvetch*
crazy	*craiceailte*	*meshuggeneh*

WHAT IS IT?

1. *bren,* "person of great energy" Irish ❏ Yiddish ❏
2. *broigas,* "petty squabbles Irish ❏ Yiddish ❏
3. *broghach,* "dirty" Irish ❏ Yiddish ❏
4. *iata,* "constipated" Irish ❏ Yiddish ❏
5. *tuathalach,* "counter-clockwise" Irish ❏ Yiddish ❏
6. *riboyne shel o'lem,* "end of the world" Irish ❏ Yiddish ❏

(3, 4, and 5 are Irish)

CHAPTER 4

✿

HOW TO LOOK IRISH

God, we simply must dress the character.

ATTIRE

Over the eons, the Irish dress code has changed in some respects, but remained constant in others. So, while Celtic (male) warriors may no longer go into battle stark naked, "Irish women and girls, down to the very little ones, always wore long skirts"—or so attests folklorist Kevin Danaher (In Ireland Long Ago). Some richly elaborate costumes were worn by the heroes and heroines of the Celtic myth cycles. "And it was in his rich clothes Cuchulain went out that day, his crimson, five-colored tunic, and his broach of inlaid gold, and his white hooded shirt, that was embroidered with red  gold." Queen Maeve, likewise, had a penchant for overdressing, sporting large gold birds on the shoulders of her purple cloak.

But by the time the English showed up, the Irish had let things slide, fashionwise. "Their external characteristics of beard and dress...are so barbarous they cannot be said to have any culture," reported Giraldus Cambrensis in 1187.

The invading Normans were also astonished to discover that, except on special occasions, not even the Irish nobility wore shoes. The only item of Hibernian couture to capture the English fancy was the *bratt*—the ankle-length, brightly colored woolen cloak worn by Irish men and women. "A fit house for an outlaw, a meet bed for a rebel, and an apt cloak for a thief," Spenser called it. In 1502, 2,320 of these garments were exported to Bristol.

But, from the time of Saint Patrick's arrival until the Age of Elizabeth, it would appear that the best-dressed and most style conscious of the Irish were priests; in fact, in 664, the Irish clergy engaged in an unseemly dustup with the Roman authorities on the subject of hairstyles. Under Holy Obedience, the monks of Ireland were eventually obliged to abandon the Celtic tonsure, hair shaved across the front of the head, in favor of the European form, a circular fringe around the crown.

Time out of mind, Irish laymen had worn their hair long, in *glibs* (ponytails). Then, in the eighteenth century, some would-be rebels began to cut their hair short. (This earned them the nickname "Croppies" from their English overlords.) So, to express your newfound Irishness, wear your tresses long and disheveled, like Bob Geldof, or shorn, à la Sinéad.

An Englishman at the end of the seventeenth century was shocked by the technique Irish women used to "highlight" their hair, observing that they "doe wash it in a lee made with stale urine and ashes, and after in water to take away the smell, by which their locks are of a burnt yellow colour much in vogue among them."

In 1960, with De Valera out and Aer Lingus jets bringing in Yankee tourists, a new day dawned, and a new women's hair-

style became general all over Ireland: the crimped "body perm," like the potato before it, was a gift from the New World.

In response to the diurnal and nocturnal downpours for which their land is celebrated, Irish men have always worn hats: bowlers for the politicians; flat tweed caps for the working class and the gunmen of the IRA; black silk top hats for the gentry; green felt ones adorned with brass buckles for Leprechauns. (In a fit of paranoia, pundit Gary Wills has posed that candidate John F. Kennedy refused to wear a hat to *distance* himself from his Irishness.)

The women of Ireland have defended themselves against the same gruesome climate by means of either long hooded cloaks, or shawls. (In Irish slang, old women are *shawlies*).

These garments are essential to the Irishwoman's traditional image, imparting as they do an air of both mystery and misery. Since World War II, the shawl has been replaced by a kerchief, tightly knotted and preferably in beige, or the pleated plastic rain hat which folds nicely into the pocketbook.

The dramatic long Kinsale cloak offered in many a catalogue doesn't travel well. In America, its wearer doesn't look like Cathleen ni Houlihan. She looks batty. The "Irish kilt," advertised as a "traditional" Irish item, is too utterly bogus to be affected by even the most stagestruck of Stage Irish.

The mere mention of the word *shift* on the stage of the Abbey Theatre once caused a riot in Dublin—so we will not speak here of undergarments, except to advise gentlemen passing for Irish against the wearing of thong briefs, and to remind the ladies that, among the Irish, "Victoria's Secret" refers to the fact that, in 1845, the queen of England could have relieved the famine, but chose not to.

HOW THE IRISH SAVED KITSCH
✍ Part One ✍

The Irish have always been fond of tchotchkes, gee-gaws, knickknacks, costume jewelry, ornaments, and accessories. In modern Ireland, the memorabilia trade is big business— the manufacturing and exporting of Waterford crystal, Belleek china, claddagh rings (and the Waterford ring holders that go with them), claddagh door knockers, Tara brooches,

stone Celtic crosses, wicker "St. Bridget's" crosses, blackthorn shillelaghs, statues of leprechauns, statutes of little boys that look like leprechauns and have a pig for a faithful friend, maps of Irish clans or "Irish Blessings" ("May the road rise up," etc.) on linen dish towels, made-in-China china jaunting cars and turf-bearing donkeys, lapel pins of the U.S. flag and the Irish flag crisscrossed, family-crest door knockers, CDs of "drinking songs," and so on.

♆ ☕ ☠ In America, any or all of these items may be collected and displayed by the Stage and/or Shanty Irish—with the exception of Waterford crystal, which is much favored by the Lace-Curtain crowd.

The Aran Sweater

It's only the stingiest of tourists who leave Ireland without one of these "classic" Irish garments, which didn't, in fact, make an appearance on the Aran Islands until the 1920s—and then by way of the Scottish coast. (Although descendants of County Kildare native John J. O'Shea claim that, in a burst of inspiration, he invented the sweater in 1850.)

Young island boys would use the event of their First Communion to debut their new sweaters, all knitted in their families' unique patterns, some with such fanciful names as the Little Bird's Eye or the Crooked Road. These intricate designs were functional as well, since the washed-up corpse of a drowned fisherman was otherwise difficult to identify. Knitting sweaters became the communal activity of the island women, many of whom would shamefully pinch pattern designs off their neighbors at Sunday Mass.

When Aran sweaters were first exported to the United States in the 1950s, they flopped, due to being available only in limited sizes—the natives could only knit sweaters to fit their husbands or sons. Today Aran knits are exported worldwide, but especially to North America and France, where they're known as *le Style Irlandais*.

☙ Stage Irish stick with the standard snowy white Aran sweater while ♨ Lace-Curtainers have moved on to other deeper, darker colors in both sweaters and rugs. ♨ Shanty Irish fancy the saucy Aran tam and matching scarf.

Celtic Crosses

A cross with encircled arms is one of Ireland's emblems. It is sometimes known as the cross of Iona, because Saint Columcille in his exile caused large stone versions to be erected on that barren island. In Ireland itself, many stone installations, adorned with typically Celtic ornamental work, date as far back as the seventh century. They are known as "high crosses." Various neopagans insist the symbol itself predates Christianity, and has something to do with naughtiness—male potency, female power, whatever.

♨ ☙ 🐷 As costume jewelry, Celtic crosses are eschewed by both the Stage and Lace-Curtain Irish, and favored by the Shanty—although all three groups are happy enough to be buried beneath them.

Claddagh

♨ ☙ 🐷 The Stage Irish wear a steroid version of this ornament, which resembles an outsize golden Buck Rogers secret decoder ring. The Lace-Curtain variety is more discreet, and sometimes inset with white gems, while their Shanty Irish kinsmen and women make due with a humble silver little thing.

But sporting a claddagh ring is no longer a sure sign of being Irish. Perhaps their popularity has something to do with utility. A ring worn on the left hand with the heart facing inward tells the world that the wearer is committed to another, whereas a ring worn with the heart facing out means, well…Hiya, sailor!

The history of the claddagh is likewise subject to variation. In one version, a sixteenth-century Galway girl fell for a Spanish sailor who had survived the wreck of the Armada. Likewise smitten, he fashioned the first claddagh ring for her, the heart, crown, and hands symbolizing (so he said) love, loyalty, and friendship. Another legend has it that a Galway man, Richard Joyce, created the ring to celebrate his escape from some pirates. If so, he must have visited points south, for museums in Spain display ancient Moorish rings almost identical to the claddagh.

Whatever its origin, the claddagh design has transcended the ring and moved on to adorn doormats, record labels, napkin rings, and, most recently, toilet paper holders.

Shillelaghs

Near the County Wicklow town still called Shillelagh once stood a forest of oak, from which a suitable "sprig of shillelagh" might be cut to serve a man for a walking stick or a sturdy weapon in a "faction fight." (In these traditional, semi-sporting combats, which might occur between aggrieved individuals or hereditarily hostile groups, the shillelagh was never swung like a club, but grasped with both hands in the middle. The knob end was employed to strike, and the other end to parry.)

But Ireland's forests, oaken and otherwise, were long ago harvested for the practical purposes of the conquering Saxons, and thereafter an Irishman's walking stick/weapon must needs be a branch plucked from a blackthorn hedge.

Shillelaghs, as stage props, were long brandished by jigging, winking vaudeville performers, and continue to appear in the mitts of Stage Irishmen—straight from the Duty Free at Shannon. In the New World, a hurlable brick soon replaced the shillelagh as the Shanty Irish weapon of choice. But the Lace-Curtain Irish's curious fondness for riding crops may just be atavistic.

Shamrocks

A small, green three-leafed plant is universally recognized as a symbol of Ireland. Its name is derived from the modern Gaelic *seamrog*, which is a diminutive of the Middle Irish *seamar*. But what, exactly, is it?

The shamrock may, or may not, be a species of clover—either white clover (*Trifolium repens)* or suckling clover, aka yellow trefoil (*Trifolium dubium*); or perhaps it is black medick (*Medicago lupilina*); or maybe wood sorrel (*Oxalis acetosella*), which is sometimes known as "lady's sorrel." The latter, in any event, is the weed annually shipped in great abundance from Ireland to America in time for March 17.

Snotty English chroniclers of the sixteenth and seventeenth centuries (such as Spenser and Holinshed) spelled it many queer ways, but identified it with watercress, upon which the (starving) Irish allegedly "feasted."

It has a quaint and false religious significance—according to pious legend, the newly arrived St. Patrick plucked a three-leafed plant from the ground at his feet and used it to illustrate the doctrine of the Trinity, thus at a stroke converting to the Faith the fierce pagan high king Leary and all his people.

As early as 1726, there is an (English) account of "This Plant worn by the [Irish] people upon St Patrick's Day…when they often commit Excess of Liquor." In the late eighteenth century, the shamrock was incorporated, by the British crown, into the insignia of the Order of Saint Patrick but it came to be identified as a symbol of radical Irish nationalism when it was taken as their battle emblem by the Volunteers in 1798, and members of Queen Victoria's Irish regiments were subsequently forbidden to wear sprigs of it.

In New York City, a weekly magazine, The *Shamrock*, or *Hibernian Chronicle*, was first published in 1810; for generations, Irish-American parochial schoolchildren were obliged each St. Patrick's day to croon a mawkish tribute to "the dear little, green little, sweet little shamrock of Ireland."

N.B.: Four-leaf clovers are proverbially lucky, and the Irish are proverbially lucky, but a shamrock has only three leaves.

☙ The Stage Irish, it goes without saying, cannot acquire or display enough shamrock-bedecked paraphernalia, from lawn ornaments to T-shirts, and they annually festoon their bosoms with bushels of the stuff.

🐷 The Shanty Irish prefer their shamrocks as dainty adornments on their Belleek porcelain dustables, or festooned in chains carefully cut from green construction paper by tiny hands.

♔ The Lace-Curtainers don't want to hear about it.

HYGIENE

In Irish poet James Stephens's exceedingly fey novel *The Crock of Gold*, a philosopher thus disparages the "extraordinary custom" of washing: "Any fool can wash himself, but every wise man knows that it is an unnecessary labor, for nature will quickly reduce him to a natural and healthy dirtiness again."

Ireland has long been known—for olfactory as well as meteorological reasons—as the "Urinal of the Planets." Its capital city glories in the sobriquet of "Dear Dirty Dublin." The river that flows through it, the Guinness stout–brown Liffey, was until recently rich with human waste—Oliver St. John Gogarty, who was once obliged to swim across it, maintained that he had "just gone through the movements."

Anyone who has spent time at close quarters in the musty funk of spilled liquor, tobacco smoke, mutton grease, beer farts, and wet wool, not to mention the pervasive miasma of B.O., that together compose the distinctive atmosphere of an Irish pub can scarcely stomach the irony of those Irish Spring soap commercials.

When passing for Irish, you are advised to go easy on the deodorant as well as the shampoo; dandruff is *de rigeur*.

This casual attention toward personal grooming transcends Irish types or, if you will, classes. But only members of the Lace-Curtain set sport a full set of teeth.

A few words about color: The ancient Irish preferred their cloaks dyed red, and red is the color of "St. Patrick's cross" in the Union Jack flag. We know that Dublinmen of Tudor times wore saffron yellow shirts, because Henry VIII outlawed the practice. Blue was long (until 1803) Ireland's official national color. Green, symbolizing death in the Celtic mind, is still considered by some of the native Irish to be unlucky. Orange should always be worn with care.

DUTY-FREE CHIC

Stage Male

Stage Female

Fly-fishing gear

Lace-Curtain Male

"Ballybunnion" rain hat

Aran pullover sweater

Green necktie

Aran knit tam

Claddagh ring

Donegal tweed golf cap

blackthorn walking st

Drinks
His Guiness
Her Bailey's

Plastic shillelagh

Tis himself

Tis herself

Aer Lingus

RASHERS

Frank Patterson

PEAT BRIQUETTES

In luggage
Rashers
Frank Patterson CD
Pack o' peat

Irish Wolfhound "Cuchulainn"

Irish Setter "Kelly"

Lace-Curtain Female

Shanty Male

Shanty Female

Drinks
Both
ck Bush

100% lambswool Kinsale
hooded cloak

Drinks
His
Bud
Her
cup o' tea

100% acrylic Claddagh
Galway shawl

Celtic knot
brooch

Knock
rosary

FIRST CLASS

Salmon

O'dyssey
TOURS

Richie
O'Shea

IRELAND

ALA
STE
AU

Bewley's

In (matched) luggage
Smoked salmon

Irish Terrier
"Buddy"

In shopping bag
St. Bridget's cross
Loaf of soda bread
Bottle of Alanna
steak sauce

CHAPTER 5

❦

HOW TO EAT IRISH
Gulp. Grub. Gulp. Gobstuff.

The Great Hunger is not only the name given to the agony of the Irish population during the potato famine, but to the condition of many a tourist in Ireland to this day.

Early in the seventeenth century, the sensitive English poet (and Irish landlord) Edmund Spenser had recommended to the British government a policy of genocide by starvation—urging that the rebellious Irish be denied food until they were forced to resort to cannibalism. A century later, the Irish patriot-satirist Jonathan Swift made "A Modest Proposal" to the same effect, but Her Majesty's government did not get around to implementing the program until the mid-1840s.

The Irish take great pride in their historic feats of anorexia: the insulted Druid bard Seanahan starved himself to death upon the king's threshold; the beloved St. Columcille would eat only nettle broth; Irish nationhood has often been asserted by "hunger strikers," from Terence MacSwiney to Bobby Sands; and Matt Talbot, the pious founder of the teetotal Pioneers, subsisted on bread and water.

Although the Irish gentry have always eaten well—from

the gluttonous royal blowouts recounted in the Celtic myth cycles to the ten-course high teas ingested by the Ascendancy—the Plain People of Ireland have always eaten Plain Food, and as little of that as necessary.

Their cuisine follows a few simple rules: 1) Eat, to the best of your ability, only starches. 2) Overcook all vegetables to achieve a homogenous pale yellow color and wet, mushy texture. 3) Overcook all meats to achieve a gray-brown color and the consistency of an old wallet. 4) If you're all out of spuds, have a turnip for breakfast. 5) Otherwise, hot milk poured on American cornflakes starts the day off right. 6) Hold over the grease in your skillet for the next meal, or the next day (tip: lamb grease has special staying power).

SPUDS

Potatoes—in Gaelic, *pratas* (pronounced, for no apparent reason, "pray-tees")—are nutritious tubers of the nightshade family, related to the tomato and tobacco. Native to South America, they were introduced to continental Europe by returning Spanish conquistadors, and (legend has it) to Ire-land, circa 1610, by Sir Walter Raleigh, who planted some on the estate in County Cork that Good Queen Bess had been kind enough to liberate on his behalf from the indigenous barbarians. The potato returned to the New World in 1719, when a crop was planted in Londonderry, New Hampshire, by immigrant Ulstermen.

"Irish potatoes," they were called, because, by then, the potato had become the Irish peasants' crop of choice—for many reasons, most of them economic. A tenant farm was likely a small one, and, per acre, potatoes yield more energy—in protein, sugar, and vitamins—than do grains. Furthermore, potatoes could actually grow in the rocky or boggy land to which the natives were confined, and a subterranean potato crop might just survive the all-too-frequent tramplings of British soldiers and foxhunting landlords.

Varieties once included the soggy but large and prolific Lumper, or Horse Potato, much favored by the poor. The gentry nowadays prefer Aran Banners, Cobbers, Dunbar Rovers, Golden Wonders, Home Guards, Irish Queens, Kerr's Pinks, Skerry Champions, and Ulster Chieftains.

Each native of Ireland eats an annual 286 pounds of spuds. Among the traditional spud-based Irish dishes are:

champ: mashed potatoes with milk, butter, and leeks or spring onions. A nettle topping is optional.

colcannon: Champ, with cabbage or kale added. When served on Halloween, may contain coins.

boxty: griddle cakes, combining grated and mashed potatoes.

boxty dumplings: dumpling-shaped boxty pudding.

Croagh Patrick potatoes: baked potatoes stuffed with bacon, cream, and cheese. (A rich-enough dish named after a spartan pilgrimage site.)

farls: potato pancakes with brown sugar added (another Halloween tradition).

fleatair: potato pancakes, straight up.

flounce: a pie of layered onions and potatoes.

oriel potatoes: mashed potatoes with egg yolk and chervil.

poundies: mashed potatoes beaten with a wooden spoon.

pig haggis: pig's intestine, stuffed with onions and mashed potatoes.

scones: buns, made with mashed potatoes (skin on) and oatmeal.

stampy: griddle cakes of grated (and drained) potatoes, mixed with flour.

tara royal: cooked potatoes with ham and egg yolks, molded into pear shapes and coated with bread crumbs.

thump: champ, with added carrots, peas, and canned corned beef.

BEYOND CORNED BEEF AND
IRISH STEW—
BUT NOT MUCH

In America, this watery and malodorous dish is the cliché St. Patrick's Day feast. Brian D. Cooper, editor of the 1990 *Irish American Handbook*, sniffs that "although it is considered quintessentially Irish fare in the U.S., this combination is virtually unknown in Ireland." Mr. Cooper's expertise notwithstanding, "corned and cabbage" is one of the restaurant dishes ordered in the Lestrygonian chapter of Joyce's *Ulysses*. (Incidentally, the Roman emperor Claudius was so fond of corned beef and cabbage that he once convoked the Senate and obliged them to declare it the tastiest of all dishes.)

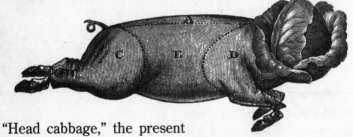

"Head cabbage," the present popular variety, is not native to Ireland; it was introduced late in the seventeenth century.

It is in fact bacon (not corned beef) and cabbage that might claim the title of Ireland's national dish. Understand: in Ireland, all pork is called bacon, except for the pig's leg, which is a "ham." And slices of what we call bacon are known as "rashers." To produce bacon and cabbage, a "joint" of bacon (sometimes "greenback," that is, unsmoked bacon) is boiled (for hours) with the cabbage, then served (with the liquid) over boiled, mashed "swedes," that is, turnips. Mmmm, that's *grand*!

Irish Stew

The other inevitable March 17 festive entree consists of five alternating layers of onions, lamb—or mutton—and potatoes. "A nourishing and economical dish, if a little indigestible. All honor to the land it has brought before the world," observed Samuel Beckett's *Molloy*. Originally, the meat component of an Irish stew was goat, since woolbearing sheep were much too valuable for farmers to eat, but billy-goat kids were expendable. Among the cookbook writers, debate yet rages as to whether carrots and/or turnips are authentic to this dish—but all are agreed that the top layer *must* be of potatoes.

Oxtail Soup

When the French were in the midst of their own famine, they endured this dish by necessity. But when it made its way over to France's less snooty neighbor, oxtail soup became a delicacy in the pantheon of Irish cuisine. Today, while somewhat out of fashion, the dish is still a must in middle-class eating establishments. Ideally the chef must use four pounds of the actual tail or, in a pinch, the spinal column of an ox. This dainty item is immersed in water, onion, flour, oil, and, in a tip of the hat to the French, a bay leaf, and voila!

Soda Bread

Why have the Irish traditionally leavened their bread with baking soda rather than yeast? Is it because they had other, better uses for yeast? Slathered with a sufficiency of butter and jam, soda bread is more or less edible. And picking out the raisins gives you something to do with your hands.

Fried Bread and Miscellaneous Horrors

For fried bread the best bread—only sliced white bread will do—is fried, preferably in rasher grease, though in a pinch any "chop" grease will do. For a gourmet touch, the edges should be slightly burned.

Coddle, a Dublin treat, is Irish stew made with sausage rather than mutton. Dulse, or dillisk, an iodine-bitter red-brown seaweed, is considered a snack food in the west, as is Irish moss, an algae allegedly high in vitamins. Crubeen—pig's feet (only the rear trotters, mind!)—is a local favorite in Cork, as are drisheens, sausages of sheep's blood. Pig's blood sausages, known as black pudding, are a breakfast favorite everywhere in Ireland. Pig's face and cabbage is…just what it sounds like.

Bird pudding is not, fortunately, what it sounds like, but is a white, watery dessert.

To those Americans passing for Stage Irish, we recommend the ostentatious ingestion of corned beef and cabbage. Irish stew will do for the Shanties. Lace-Curtain Irish usually have someone else—preferably not of Irish extraction—do their cooking for them.

NO FREE LUNCH

With a well-deserved international reputation for bad meals badly served, it is…ironic to say the least that, in the New World, the Irish were—and are—to be found in great numbers in the restaurant trade.

In the last century, Irish immigrant girls often found work as maids in the homes of the wealthy. (In 1860, seventy thousand colleens were employed as domestic servants in New York City and Brooklyn.) Some of them may have gained a rudimentary knowledge of preparing food other than potatoes by methods other than boiling, but the "aristocrats" for whom they were cooking were all rubes themselves. Today, because the "hospitality industry" likewise employs unskilled labor, no Green Card questions asked, Irish girls newly arrived in the New World often become waitresses.

Back then, as now, Irish lads just off the boat sometimes found work tending bar in the saloons that were owned by Irish lads who'd got off the boat before them. In 1871, there were 7,500 licensed "grog shops" in New York City. Many of them—the ones that weren't German—were Irish. In some of them, food—of a sort—was served. There was, for instance, a saloon on Nineteenth Street and Avenue C, owned by Charles F. Murphy, the last Tammany leader. There a "lunch" for the workingman—a bowl of soup and a glass of beer—cost a nickel. In others, such as Chicago alderman Hinky Dink McKenna's bar in the Alaska Hotel, "lunch" was free. (The newly urbanized Irish were used to coming in from the fields at midday to eat "dinner," and had to get used to the very idea of "lunch.")

The institution known as a restaurant is actually a rather recent invention, and the self-consciously "ethnic" or "theme" restaurant even more recent. Today, in many American cities, you can dine in spanking new, lavishly decorated, utterly ersatz "Irish" restaurants—often occupying the sites of recently demolished authentic Irish barrooms—and there is no free lunch.

CHAPTER 6

✧

HOW TO DRINK IRISH

We'll have a gorgeous drunk to astonish the druidy druids.

One of the most offensive stereotypes—at which you, when passing for Irish, are obliged to take continuous, loud offense—is that of the drunken Irishman. In truth, the Irish do not drink as much (per capita) as either the English or the Germans—because not all the Irish are "on the drink." Many folk in the North are booze-loathing Presbyterians; many Catholics in the republic have "taken the pledge" and are teetotal, pin-wearing Pioneers—deeply committed, evangelical nondrinkers (and thus even more boringly obsessed with alcohol than the alcoholics). The novelist Honor Tracy warned, "I would always recommend caution in dealing with an Irish teetotaler. There never was a Pioneer but was a bastard at heart."

The first Alcoholics Anonymous chapter in Europe was Dublin's, formed in 1946.

The ancient Celts were a cattle-herding people, very similar, except in stature, to the Masai of Africa, and like them, when in need of a pick-me-up, often quaffed a refreshing mixture of milk and (hot) cow's blood. (It was alleged that the newly arrived Irish in New York's nineteenth-century tenements frequented neighborhood slaughterhouses for fresh blood to drink.) Nevertheless, we have it on the authority of many ancient Irish tales, as well as the word of the Roman historian Tacitus, that the Celts also drank ale.

A PINT OF PLAIN

▨

"Do you know what I am going to tell you," he said, with his wry mouth. "A pint of plain is your only man."—Flann O'Brien, *At Swim-Two-Birds*.

Ale, a brew of water, yeast, and barley malt, was invented in Egypt. In medieval Ireland, as elsewhere in Europe, it was usually a product of the monasteries, where (we read) "the fermented barley malt was boiled with aromatic herbs of oak bark and brewed in oaken vats." In the *Hisperica Famina*, an anonymous seventh-century monk rejoiced to recall how at the end of a journey, "we thirstily drank our fill of the joy-giving ale." Bridget, Ireland's patron saint, was famed for her brewing skills. To her is attributed a (tenth-century?) poem in Gaelic:

> *I should like to have a great lake of ale*
> *For the King of Kings.*
> *I should like the whole of the Heavenly Host*
> *To be drinking it for all eternity.*

In days of old, ale was usually drunk hot, and flavored with spices. When mixed with honey, it was known as braget.

A style of cheap, dark beer called porter (because it was preferred by the laboring class) was first produced and drunk in London, circa 1700, and so was a stronger variety, called "stout porter," or, simply, "stout." In 1787, Dublin brewer Arthur Guinness began producing both Plain Porter for domestic consumption and Double Stout for export. His son perfected the recipe—by accident, according to a legend about a bishop and a banquet—and it's roasted barley that still gives the brew its distinctive taste and "dark fantastic" color.

In Ireland, Guinness had, and has, rivals, including Murphy's and Beamish, two brands from Cork. But by the mid nineteenth century Guinness was outselling all other Irish stouts combined; by 1900 it had become the largest brewery in Europe.

In American saloons, a mixture of lager beer and stout, known as a Black and Tan, is sometimes ordered by those passing for Irish. Since Black and Tans was the name given to the British irregulars once hired to hunt down and murder the Irish, this practice is to be deplored. Imagine, if you will, an Israeli ordering a pint of Gestapo.

"Pulling" or "building"—that is, pouring—a pint of stout is allegedly an art and a science, and you can gain bonus Stage Irish points by blathering on about it. The Guinness company, however, recently spent £8 million teaching British bartenders to do it "the Irish way."

Let the last word on pouring stout—indeed, the last word on everything—belong to Joyce. Behold HCE, the tavern keeper hero of *Finnegans Wake*, "unbulging an o'connell's, the true one, all seethic, a luckybock, pledge of the stoup... pressures be to our hoary frother, the pop gave his sullen bulletaction and, bilge, sled a movement of cathartic emulsipotion down the sloppery slide of a slaunty to tilted lift-ye-landsmen."

🎩 👒 🐷 When passing for Irish, it is essential that you invariably order a "pint," i.e., a large glass of stout, and, upon tasting it, observe that, like some fine wines, Guinness doesn't "travel well." The finest pint you ever had was in a little snug in Dublin, etc.

🎩 The Lace-Curtain Irish are loath to drink anything as proletarian as beer, save after a vigorous bout of squash, when they prefer a Czech lager. On ceremonial occasions, they may partake of a glass of stout with the addition of four ounces of champagne, a beverage known as a Black Velvet.

🐷 Shanty Irishmen buy stout by the pint, and by the round, and expect you to buy a round in return. The brand they prefer—if they are feeling aggressively Catholic—will be neither the Prod-produced Beamish nor Guinness, but the Papist-made Murphy's.

👒 Those aspiring to the Stage Irish condition are advised to follow the example of Senator "Pat" Moynihan on a recent St. Patrick's Day morn, hoisting a pint and bellowing, "First Today!" (which earned him forever that sobriquet from columnist Jimmy Breslin).

THE OLD STAND

❧

"The pub is first and foremost a refuge, a safe haven where a person can meet friends and forget about the headaches and problems of work, home, the past, the future," explains Anthony Bluett in *Things Irish*.

In Ireland, pubs are ubiquitous. There's not the smallest town without two or three, and according to a 1925 government report, 191 towns had "an excessive number" of them. As for the cities, Mr. Bloom rightly believed you couldn't make your way across Dublin without passing one. ("Pub," by the way, is a Victorian English slang abbreviation for the much older "public house." In Irish, such an establishment was long known as an "alehouse" or, in Gaelic, a tabhairne—pronounced, as you might expect, "tavern.")

The ancient Brehon laws of Celtic Ireland contained most-specific regulations concerning the brewing of ale for sale and the running of the alehouses, known then as bruideans.

The invading English—at home no mean brewers and drinkers of ale—couldn't get over the shock of the Irish fondness for a glass. Richard Lawrence, a political economist who accompanied Cromwell to Ireland, set his mind in 1682 to calculating the financial loss resulting from the national weakness:

	Number Per Parish	Cost Per Individual	Number of Parishes	Total in £
Wine-bibbers	3	10£	2,500	75,000
Ale-topers	5	4£	2,500	50,000
Fuddlicups	?	10£	2,500	25,000
Tapsters and Drawers		Cost to country per annum		4,000
		Loss through bad work of the sots per annum		20,000

Despite their Puritan over-lords, the tapsters and drawers of Ireland have continued to ply their trade.

To pass for Irish, you must have a "local"—a favorite pub which is, according to you, more "authentic" than all the others (with which it is, in fact, identical). Because a feature of Irish pub culture is craic—that is, conversa-tion—pub purists deplore the presence of either a television set or a jukebox (the latter defined by Oliver St. John Gogarty as "an illu-minated coal scuttle"). But in the evenings, live (preferably tradi-tional) music is tolerated.

The presence of female per-sons in a pub was once a scandal. But today, even in rural Ireland, the absence of customers of the fair sex should be taken as a bad sign.

McLAREN & Cº
DUBLIN

PUBS, *Historical*

Brazen Head on Bridge Street, the oldest licensed—since 1666—pub in Dublin.

Davy Byrne's Moral Pub in Dublin, in which Mr. Leopold Bloom famously lunched on Gorgonzola cheese and burgundy wine. Now relocated and refurbished, it is by no means what it was.

Dooley's Merchant Exchange Hotel on Boston's State Street, meeting place since 1846 of the Hub's Irish "benevolent societies." Just down the street is the Bunch of Grapes, an even older tavern favored by George Washington.

Finnegans Wake, one of many "traditional Irish" pubs now flourishing in Paris.

The Lone Star Saloon and Palm Garden, at the south end of Chicago's Whiskey Row, where barkeep Mickey Finn plied his nefarious trade, aided by his part-ner-in-crime Kate Rose Flynn.

McGillian's, since 1860 an Irish oasis on Drury Lane in Philadel-phia's city center.

McSorley's Old Ale House, justly designated as "wonderful" by author Joe Mitchell, which was opened in New York City in 1854 by the Irish Quaker John McSorley and is still going strong.

In Irish America, the infamous corner saloon evolved from the tenement-neighborhood grocery store, which sold beer by the bucket. When Prohibition transformed drinking into a popular and sophisticated pastime, those saloons became "speakeasies," or "gin mills," in which abominations known as "cocktails" were served. These establishments, upon repeal, became the chic "bars," or (God help us) "beverage lounges" that are, even as we speak, being transformed into "saloons" or "traditional Irish pubs," frequented by the likes of us.

PUBS, *Mythological*

Cheers, a sitcom pub in sitcom Boston, which spawned a real-life pub by the same name in that very city.

Duffy's Tavern mise en scene of a long-running weekly radio comedy. "Archie the manager speaking, Duffy ain't here."

Dinty Moore's the suds-and corned-beef emporium of which Jiggs, in the comic strip "Bringing Up Father," dreamed, while snoozing at the opera.

The nameless saloon to which viewers were often welcomed by Jackie Gleason, in the persona of Joe the Bartender. "You just missed Crazy Guggenheim."

The Saloon on Archey Road (South Side Chicago) owned and operated by Mr. Martin Dooley, the alter ego of author Finley Peter Dunne.

The End of the Line Cafe, setting of Eugene O'Neill's *The Iceman Cometh*, which was based on Jimmy the Priest's (a bar on Fulton Street in New York.)

THE WATER OF LIFE

From an apocryphal Irish sermon: "It's whiskey makes you bate your wives; it's whiskey makes your homes desolate; it's whiskey makes you shoot your landlords—and it's whiskey that makes you miss them."

Whiskey is, in effect, distilled ale. The Arabs, of all people, are thought to have invented it. In pious legend, it was St. Patrick himself who taught the Irish the art of distilling; but Irish whiskey (always spelled with an e) first enters recorded history in the *Annals of the Four Masters,* 1405, wherein we learn that one Richard Mac Raghnaill of Leitrim died of an overdose of it. Originally employed as a medicine, *usque baugh* (the water of life) was often flavored with licorice, and usually drunk hot. One medieval punch, known as *scailtin,* contained whiskey, hot milk, butter, sugar, and cinnamon or cloves.

It has been argued—and, when passing for Irish, you *will* argue—that the Irish taught the Scots the art of distilling. But to this day, most Irish "whiskey" is manufactured differently from Scotch "whisky." As a rule, the Irish do *not* expose the malt to peat smoke during roasting, and they usually triple-distill it, whereas Scotch is distilled only twice.

In 1800, there were two thousand legal stills operating in Ireland; by 1900, no fewer than four hundred brands of Irish whiskey were offered for sale in the United States. Then, in the 1920s, Ireland's ongoing war with England and the onset of Prohibition in the USA entirely eliminated the industry's foreign markets. And—thanks in part to the efforts of bootlegger Old Joe Kennedy—Americans turned to Scotch. Farewell, then, to Allman's, Coleraine, Old Comber, Locke's, Kilbeggan, and even the legendary Tullamore Dew.

Ireland's few surviving whiskey makers were forced to consolidate, and formed the Irish Distillers Group. In 1986 ownership of the IDG—Powers, Jameson, Bushmill's and all—passed, for $525 million, to the snooty French hooch cartel of Pernod Ricard.

There is, however, hope.

In 1989, John Teeling, an Irish-born Harvard Business School graduate, began production of "real" Irish whiskey at a defunct distillery in Dundalk that he christened Cooley. Author and whiskey authority Jim Murray recently praised Connemara, Cooley's pure pot-still, peated single malt, as "wondrous, top-rank, brilliant." It would require excessive Irish begrudgery not to wish Teeling's enterprise well.

While exported Jameson's remains the world's favorite Irish whiskey, the natives prefer Powers, or, when they can get it, Red Breast, a twelve-year-old 80-proof tipple so splendid it is known as the "priest's bottle." But these days, the Irish often drink Ballygowan sparkling water or, when indulging in the hard stuff, the similarly made-in-Ireland Celtic vodka.

Mixology

Top-of-the-line Irish whiskey (such as Powers or Black Bush) is best taken straight, or with a couple of fingers of cool water added. Never on the rocks—and, for the love of God, hold the soda. Nonetheless, American bartenders have, over the years, concocted several "Irish" cocktails.

- A **Manhattan** made with Irish whiskey (instead of Scotch) is a Rory O'More.

- An Irish-whiskey-based **Tom Collins** is a Mike Collins.

- **Irish Mist** is a venerable liqueur which lists honey as one of its ingredients. Mixed half-and-half with Irish whiskey, it makes an Irish Brogue.

- **Bailey's Irish Cream** is the best-selling liqueur in the world. (It is manufactured, in London, by Gilbey's.) It is not so much a drink as a dessert. When combined with brandy and crème de menthe, it is known as an Irish Flag.

- A **straight shot of whiskey** taken with a beer chaser was a favorite of the (Irish) miners of Butte, Montana. We call it a **boilermaker**. They called it a Shawn O'Farrell.

- **Irish coffee**, invented by Joe Sheridan, the bartender at Shannon Airport, briefly became something of a craze in suburban America. Should you undertake to prepare a batch, you are advised to follow the example of Mr. Sheridan, and employ one of the cheaper whiskey brands. (Note: A journalist named Stanton Delaplane maintains he invented Irish coffee in San Francisco's Buena Vista Bar.)

We note without comment the existence of the **Scarlett O'Hara** (Southern Comfort and grenadine) and the **Screaming Banshee**, which contains vodka, cream, crème de menthe, and crème de banane.

 The Stage Irish must invariably refer to whiskey as either "a drop of the cray-tshur" or "a ball o' malt," and indignantly eschew Bushmills as "from the North." Lace-Curtainers, au contraire, exclusively sip Black Bush. The Shanty Irish, those of them who aren't Pioneers, aren't particular.

TOASTS AND TAY

"Traditional Irish Toasts," as featured on souvenir postcards and tea towels, are a standard part of the Stage Irish repertoire; "A fart for the bishop of Cork" was popular among Protestants circa 1690. Today, the usual Irish toast is a simple and straightforward "Good luck."

Because, if you raise and drain your glass sufficiently, the road will rise up to meet you, right enough.

"When I makes tea, I makes tea," said the proverbial Old Mother Grogan, "and when I makes water, I makes water."

Pound for pound, the Irish are the world's greatest tea drinkers. Like their neighbors the English, and unlike the rest of the civilized world, they made the switch from coffee in the eighteenth century, for reasons of economy. After the British won control of the Indian and Chinese tea trade, the stuff became irresistibly cheap; by 1880, tea had even replaced buttermilk as the drink offered to travelers in rural Ireland.

Instructions for conducting an Irish tea ceremony can be found on many a gift-shop dish towel. The teapot must be warmed ("scalded") with boiling water—which is poured out before you add the loose tea (a tad more than a teaspoon per cup) and boiling water. Stir and cover. The tea is then left to "steep," the pot snugly fitted with knitted woolen tea "cozy." Serve with (whole) milk and (plenty of) sugar, but never lemon.

Tradition be damned, tea bags are now general all over Ireland. (They were, after all, invented—in 1904, in New York—by an Irishman, Thomas Sullivan.) World-famous tea merchant Thomas Lipton was likewise born (in Glasgow) to Irish parents, but the blends the Irish prefer are Barry's of Cork or Bewley's of Dublin.

CHAPTER 7

HOW TO ACT IRISH

—I am not thinking of the offense to my mother.
—Of what then? Buck Mulligan asked.
—Of the offense to me, Stephen answered.

HAVE A THIN SKIN ON YOU

It is alleged that the Irish are a touchy lot, insecure, defensive, easily offended. This is far from the case. You will never hear an Irish man or woman wax indignant at a (typical) passage from Walden, by the patron saint of American liberals, Henry David Thoreau: "The culture of an Irishman is an enterprise to be undertaken with a sort of moral bog hoe. [He is] born not to rise in the world, he nor his posterity, till their wading webbed bog-trotting feet get *talaria* to their heels." Nor  will he or she demand their money back upon exposure to the "Celts" in the movie *Robin Hood, Prince of Thieves*, who wear animal skins, have red hair and red faces, and are alleged to "eat their young."

Rather, the Irish watch, bemused, the trailers for the blockbuster hits *Leprechaun* and *Leprechaun 2*, *Leprechaun 3*, and *Leprechaun 4: In Space* in which a vile imp jigs and sticks out his mottled green fourteen-inch tongue while croaking, "Kiss me I'm Irish."

As a class, Irish Americans have been spared slander by neither old-fashioned etiquette nor new-fangled political correctness, since they have gone from being a powerless minority who could be denigrated with impunity, to being a powerful minority, who may be insulted without giving offense.

STICKS AND STONES

In their worldwide diaspora, the Irish have been called many things by their welcoming hosts; this list of pejoratives and euphemisms is by no means complete.

barks: obsolete British slang for Irishmen, and/or persons with coughs.

bog trotters: since the seventeenth century, a common term for dwellers in, or refugees from, Ireland. "An sham of idle Irish bogtrotters" is the edifying example of usage cited in the *Oxford English Dictionary.*

boiled dinners: in New England, a dish of corned beef, cabbage, and potatoes—hence designating habitual consumers of same.

Celts: The word is Latin, and means "chisels" or "ax heads." It was first used, by the Romans, to designate the people in whose burial mounds such tools were found. (This is rather as if archaeologists of the future were to call us "Plastic Bottles.") The Celts, aka Gauls, Gaels, Galatians, Milesians, etc., came storming out of what is now southern Germany in the fifth century B.C. They swarmed across Europe, occupying France, Spain, and northern Italy. (In 390 B.C. they sacked Rome.) Sometime in the third century, they arrived in Ireland, which is one of the few places where they may still, upon occasion, be found.

chaws, chaw mouths: Chicago usage; talkative persons, complainers, boasters—thus, typical Irish.

dogans: Canadian usage; a derogatory term for Irish Catholics, from the common family name.

flannelmouths: pejorative Americanism, suggesting the stereotypical Irish qualities of insincerity, sentimentality, and boastfulness. "I ain't like those flannelmouth Micks goin' around singin' Molly Malone all the time," snarls Jimmy Cagney in the film, *The Fighting 69th.*

Greenlanders: Irishmen; gullible, ignorant persons.

harps: traditional American; the harp being one of
Ireland's ancient national symbols, to this day
appearing on the republic's coins, state seal, presi-
dential flag—and on Guinness labels. England's
King Henry VIII, of all people, was the first to adopt
it as the Irish heraldic device, or "cognizance."
Joke—Q: Who's the strongest Irishhman ever? A:
The harp that once threw Tara's Halls.

Hibernians: When used by WASPs, this term is—like
Hebrews for Jews—a patronizing euphemism.
The Irish themselves employ it only when
putting on airs. Probably it comes from
Latin—the Romans (who never went
there) slandered Ireland's famously
moderate climate by calling it Hibernia, which implies a "wintery" place;
however, in myth, Heber was the
name of the first Milesian, or Celt, to
arrive in Ireland. (He was, by the way, a direct
descendant of Japeth, son of Noah.)

mackerel snappers: American slang; people who eat
fish on Friday, hence Catholics, hence Irish.

Micks: an abbreviation of Michael, the common Irish
Christian name, honoring the biblical prince of
angels. One of the earliest recorded American uses
of this term is by the young journalist Mark Twain,
in *Roughing It*, 1872: "The Micks got to throwing
stones through the Methodis' Sunday School
windows." According to David Grote's 1992 *British
English for American Readers*, this word is "for the
most part not seen as particularly derogatory, except
of course by the Irish."

narrow backs: obsolete American slang for second-
generation Irish, who are no longer engaged or
interested in honest labor.

niggers turned inside out: a common eighteenth-century American witticism; blacks, for their part, were known as "smoked Irish."

paddies: an abbreviation of Patrick, the common Irish Christian name, honoring both the national saint and Patrick Sarsfield, patriot; in Britain, hod carriers. *Joke*—Q: What's green and sits around the swimming pool? A: Paddy O' Furniture.

Patlanders: self-explanatory.

salt water turkeys: obsolete American usage; first generation Irish, salt water suggesting just off the boat. (See Turks.)

spuds: sharp, spadelike digging tools, hence potatoes, hence potato eaters.

teagues: common eighteenth-century British usage, now archaic; from the once-common Irish name Tadhg. In a 1773 letter, Dublin-born Jonathan Swift conceded, "I am a Teague, or an Irishman, or what you please." The term is still sometimes used by Northern Irish Protestants to denote Catholics.

terriers: a reference, possibly, to the breed of dog known as the Irish terrier. Many of the laborers who built America's railroads were Irish immigrants and were collectively known as "terriers"—a word they pronounced "tarriers." According to their "theme song," called "Drill Ye Tarriers, Drill," they would "work all day/ for the sugar in your tay / down behind the railway…"

Turks: a once common derogatory American slang term for Irishmen, of obscure derivation. Possibly it is derived from *torc*, the Gaelic word for "castrated boar."

? ? ? ? ? **KELT** or **SELT** ? ? ? ? ?

The word *Celt* is derived from the Greek term for the tribes of Gaul, *Keltoi*; the Romans made it *Celtae*, and pronounced it "Keltay." In Irish, it's *Caelteach*, and the Gaelic C is always hard, that is, pronounced "K"—there is no letter *k* in the language).

Yet the *Oxford English Dictionary* prefers the pronunciation "Seltic," as do Boston basketball fans, preferring the "sibilant c"—a *c* pronounced "s" when occurring before the vowel *e*. This was a snotty French affectation, and entered the English language only after the Norman Invasion.

AS IRISH AS...

Should you ever wonder what your well-bred neighbors (in Old and/or New England) really think of you, consider the following once—or still—common figures of speech:

> **Irish** (noun): anger, bad temper, fighting spirit, e.g., the pro-Zionist American pop tune of the 1940s that declared "the Jews have got their Irish up"; (adjective): illogical.

Irish ambulance: a wheelbarrow.

Irish apple: a potato, aka bog orange; the cargo of Irish vessels was said by eighteenth-century British sailors to be "fruit and lumber"—that is, broomsticks and potatoes.

Irish applesauce: mashed potatoes.

Irish apricot: a potato.

Irish arms: thick-ankled (female) legs. As long ago as 1785, Edmund Grose, in his *Dictionary of the Vulgar Tongue*, observed, "It is said of Irish women that they have a dispensation from the Pope to wear the thick end of their legs downward."

Irish baby buggy: British; a wheelbarrow. (They worked in construction, you see.)

Irish banjo: American; a shovel.

Irish battleship: British naval; a barge.

Irish beauty: a woman with two black eyes.

Irish bouquet: a stone or rock, when used as a weapon.

Irish bridge: a culvert.

Irish bull: a figure of speech containing a contradiction in terms.

Irish coat of arms: two black eyes and a bloody nose.

Irish cherries: American lunch-counter jargon; split peas.

Irish confetti: bricks (when thrown, as weapons).

Irish curtains: cobwebs.

Irish club house: a police station.

Irish diamond: a rock.

Irish dinner: nothing to eat, a fast.

Irish dividend: American; a political shakedown.

Irish draperies: pendulous breasts.

Irish evidence: false evidence, perjury.

Irish fan: a shovel.

Irish faucet: a (nonfunctioning) tap displayed on the front lawn suggesting (falsely) that the inhabitants have running water.

Irish flag: a diaper.

Irish football: a potato.

Irish funnies: the obituary column.

Irish fortune: British, circa 1890; the female genitals and a pair of clogs.

Irish goose: a dish of codfish.

Irish grape: a potato.

Irish handcuffs: saloon slang; a beer and a shot.

Irish harp: a shovel.

Irish hint: a very broad hint.

Irish hoist: 1. a kick in the pants. 2. an awkward fall.

Irish horse: tough salted beef.

Irish hurricane: British nautical; a flat calm.

Irish inch: an erection.

Irish kiss: American; a slap in the face.

Irish lemon: a potato.

the Irish local: American; a wheelbarrow.

the Irish mail: British; a sack of potatoes.

Irish mile: considerably more than a mile.

Irish mutton: American criminal slang; syphilis.

Irish necktie: a noose.

Irish nightingale: a frog.

Irish pennant: nautical; a loose end, a dangling bit of rope.

Irish promotion: a reduction in pay.

Irish Pullman: U.S. railway slang; a handcar.

Irish raise: (See *Irish promotion.*)

Irishman's rest: going up a friend's ladder with a hod of bricks.

Irish rifle: a small comb.

Irish root: the penis.

Irish rose: rhyming slang; a nose.

Irish screwdriver: a hammer.

Irish seven-course meal: a six-pack and a potato.

Irish shave: (to take an): to defecate.

Irish spoon: a spade.

Irish theater: British military; the brig.

Irish toothache: in males, an erection; in females, pregnancy.

Irish toothpick: the penis.

Irish trick: a dirty trick.

Irish turkey: American hobo slang; corned beef and cabbage.

Irish twins: siblings born in the same year.

Irish wash: turning the tablecloth over, dirty side down.

the Irish way: heterosexual anal intercourse (curiously, because in 1990 an Irishman was sentenced to two years in prison for "sodomizing" his wife).

Irish wedding: 1. masturbation. 2. the emptying of a cesspool. (To look as if "you've danced at an Irish wedding" is to have two black eyes.)

to weep Irish: to shed insincere tears.

you're Irish: you're talking nonsense.

SCREW THE IRISH!

In one of his masterful monologues, Lenny Bruce portrayed a desperate second-rate American stand-up comic on the stage of the London Palladium. "Frank Dell" is flopping miserably, until he is inspired to shout, "Screw the Irish!" thereby bringing down (literally) the house. Knocking the Irish is a traditional Sassenach pastime. Match the Irish-basher to the slander.

1. **Matthew Arnold**
2. **The Chicago Tribune**
3. **Winston Churchill**
4. **Tom Clancy**
5. **Harry Cohn**
6. **Noël Coward**
7. **Oliver Cromwell**
8. **Benjamin Disraeli**
9. **Friedrich Engels**
10. **Lillian Hellman**
11. **Ernest Hemingway**
12. **Henry James**
13. **Murray Kempton**
14. **D. H. Lawrence**
15. **Henry Cabot Lodge**
16. **Princess Margaret**
17. **Sir Robert Peel**
18. **Ezra Pound**
19. *Punch* **magazine**
20. **Lord John Russell**
21. **William Shakespeare**
22. **Alfred, Lord Tennyson**
23. **Evelyn Waugh**

A. "All the troubles in the world are caused by Irishmen and Jews."

B. (re James Joyce): "The damned Irish, they have to moan over something or other, but you never heard of an Irishhman starving to death."

C. "Ah, the Irish. The minute one of them accomplishes anything, there's always another one behind him with a rock, waiting to bring him down."

D. "The Hibernian has the slave mentality and will act accordingly. He is a mixture of childishness and ferocity. He is basely superstitious, callous to suffering, credulous, excitable, thriftless, untruthful, dirty, pettily dishonest, destructive, cunning, imitative, tortuous, devoid of moral courage and intensely vain."

E. "There is no topic more soporific and generally boring than the topic of Ireland as Ireland, as a nation."

F. "I was deeply moved by the tragic shabbiness of this sinister country."

G. (British prime minister, on early reports of the famine): "The Irish always have a tendency to exaggerate."

H. "In what part of her body stands Ireland?" "Marry, sir, in the buttocks; I found it out by the bogs." (*The Comedy of Errors*, 5:2)

I. (British prime minister, three years into the famine): "We have subscribed, worked, visited, clothed for the Irish. The only return is rebellion and calumny. Let us not grant, lend, clothe any more and see what will happen."

J. (to the mayor of Chicago, while visiting): "The Irish are pigs. All pigs."

K. "Scratch a convict or a pauper and the chances are you will tickle the skin of an Irish Catholic."

L. "There are only two destinations for the Irish, hell or the United States."

M. "The Irish are charming, soft-voiced, quarrelsome, priest-ridden, feckless and happily devoid of the slightest integrity."

N. (the author and noted friend of the working class muttering, in 1978, about the help): "I see the little Irish girl has set out the wrong dinner plates again."

O. "Ireland is the bane of England and the opprobrium of Europe."

P. "The Irish people are undisciplinable, anarchical and turbulent by nature."

Q. "We have always found the Irish to be a bit odd. They refuse to be English."

R. "Ireland is to my mind something like the bottom of an aquarium, with little people in crannies like prawns."

S. "The blind hysterics of the Celt."

T. (his fictional hero Jack Ryan in conversation with the British Royal Family): "We Irish-Americans have made out pretty well...You have a pretty good system over here. Sooner or later, civilization wins out over barbarism."

U. (reporting his successful massacre of the citizens of Drogheda): "I am persuaded that this is the righteous judgement of God upon these barbarous wretches."

V. "The Irish have supplied England, America, and Australia with prostitutes, pimps, thieves, swindlers, beggars, and other rabble."

W. (to *Irish Times* columnist Nuala O'Faolain): "I've never wanted to go to your country. The very thought of it gives me fatigue."

HAVE A TERRIBLE TEMPER ON YOU

⚯

To "have your Irish up" is to be in a bad temper. Of the deadly sins, Wrath is the abiding vice of the Irish race, as Avarice is of the…well, never mind.

Anger often gives rise to assault and even battery, for which reason G. K. Chesterton called Ireland "the land of broken hearts, and the land of broken heads." Even the republic's official national anthem proclaims, **"We're children of a fighting race / That never yet has known disgrace / And as we march to face the foe / We'll chant a soldier's song!"**

In rural Ireland long ago, stick-swinging, rock-throwing confrontations between clans or towns, known as "faction fighting," was considered a recreational sport. In the slums of mid-nineteenth-century America, the Irish naturally partook of the customary inner-city activities of domestic violence and gang warfare, earning for themselves the collective sobriquet of the "Fighting Irish." Curiously, they adopted this insult as a boast, and what was originally a racial slander has been proudly adopted as the nickname of Notre Dame University's teams and alumni.

For the first decades of the twentieth century, Irish Americans did indeed dominate fisticuffs: boxing champions included light heavyweights George Gardner and "Philadelphia" Jack O' Brien; middleweights Tommy Ryan, Mike O'Dowd, and welterweight Jack Britton; Mickey "the Toy Bulldog" Walker; featherweights Terry McGovern and "Brooklyn" Tommy Sullivan; and bantamweights Frankie Neil and Joe Lynch.

But as prizefighters, the Irish reputation has outlived the facts. When Ulster's Barry McGuigan won the world featherweight crown in 1985, he became the first Irishman to claim a boxing title in fifty-two years. The last Irish-American heavyweight champ was James J. Braddock, who lost his title to Joe Louis in 1937.

PUBLIC ENEMIES AND DIRTY RATS

Irish immigrants to America found employment not only in the ring, but also in another field traditionally offering economic opportunities to the underclass: crime. Naturally, when they achieved some eminence in the profession, they were stereotyped as "naturals" and fit for nothing else. To pass for Irish it is necessary to evince a perverse pride in some of these Irish-American gangsters, ones Jimmy Cagney never got to play:

The Dead End Kids

The slum-tenement Five Points district of Manhattan (the area now comprising Chinatown and Little Italy) was, throughout the late nineteenth century, the stomping ground of several extremely savage all-Irish criminal gangs: the Pug Uglies; the Daybreak Boys; the Walsh Gang, headed by Jimmy "the Mick" Walsh; the Dead Rabbits, who were enforcers ("sluggers") for Tammany Hall, waging full-scale street war against the Bowery Boys, who represented the anti-Irish "Native American" party; the Tub o' Blood Bunch, featuring Skinner Meehan, Sweeny the Boy, and Brian Boru; and the Kerryonians, who were sworn to victimize only Englishmen.

The gang known as the Whyos were not as particular. "Baboon" Connelly, "Googy" Corcoran, "Dandy" Johnny Dolan, "Red Rocks" Farrell, "Bull" Hurley, "Fig" McGerald, "Piker" Ryan, and "Hoggy" Walsh were equal-opportunity thieves and killers-for-hire. Dolan seems to have been a kind of evil genius. He invented a most ingenious hand-held eye-gouging device, which enabled him to keep his pockets stuffed with his victims' eyeballs.

🔫 Richie Fitzpatrick (1880–1905) An Irish hit man in the employ of "Monk" Eastman's (otherwise all-Jewish) New York mob, Fitzpatrick actually invented the "gun in the toilet" gag, which would be made famous in the movie *The Godfather*.

🔫 Martin "Bully" Morrison (fl. 1920) The self-proclaimed "King of Hell's Kitchen" was a red-haired, red-whiskered Orangeman. In the early 1920s, he and his sons "Jock" and "Bull" stormed through New York's infamous tenement district, bashing their cowering Popish enemies with shillelaghs.

🔫 Owney "the Killer" Madden (1892–1964) A Liverpool-Irish immigrant, Owney rose to prominence with the Hell's Kitchen gang, the Gophers, and by the age of twenty-three was its leader, having bumped off five men—among them rival Little Patsy Doyle, for whose murder Madden served eight years in Sing Sing. Upon his release, reformed and newly dignified, Owney went into the rackets: bootlegging, sports promotion (he "managed" heavyweight tomato can Primo Carnera), and night clubs. As owner of Harlem's celebrated Cotton Club, the Killer took an instant dislike to the music of the Duke Ellington orchestra during its first gig there, and made his feelings known to Jimmy McHugh. McHugh rushed to the bandstand. "For God's sake play 'Mother Machree,' " he begged the Duke, "or I'm a goner!" Ellington was kind enough to comply.

🔫 Charles Dion "Deanie" O'Banion (1892–1924) The pre-Scarface boss of Chicago's underworld, an ex–altar boy from the North Side, the possessor of a sweet tenor voice, a snappy dresser and something of a wit, Deanie was also a safecracker, a bootlegger, a Democratic party enforcer, and the killer of an estimated fifty men. He steadfastly opposed Capone on the subject of opening brothels—Extramarital sex, he believed, was a sin. (A devout Catholic, he always carried a rosary on his person.)

🔫 George "Bugs" Moran (1893–1957) O'Banion's successor on Chicago's North Side and another devout Catholic, this accomplished killer also deplored prostitution—"lower than a rat's ass," he called it—and sex in general. In 1929, Bugs was the target of the St. Valentine's Day Massacre but overslept, leaving seven of his men to be gunned down by the Capone mob. His reputation never recovered.

🔫 George R. "Machine-Gun" Kelly (1895–1954) Although J. Edgar Hoover named him "Public Enemy Number One," Kelly never actually fired a shot in anger, much less killed anyone. He was, in fact, a timid sort—when surrounded, he is alleged (by Hoover) to have uttered the memorable phrase, "Don't shoot, G-Men, don't shoot!" (Jack McGurn, the other mobster nicknamed "Machine-Gun," was a genuine killer, one of Al Capone's tommy gun–wielding "soldiers" who took part in the St. Valentine's Day Massacre. But his real name was James De Mora.)

🔫 Roger Touhy (1898–1959) He and his six brothers, the sons of a Chicago policeman, were known as the "Terrible Touhys." Prohibition-era bootleggers, they produced a superior brand of beer, which they generously supplied to local politicos, in bottles with personalized labels. Unable to outmuscle the Toughys, the rival Capone mob had Roger set up for a kidnapping, of which he happened to be entirely innocent, and in 1933 he was arrested and jailed—to a loud chorus of self-congratulation from the FBI. It took twenty-five years for Roger to establish his innocence; three weeks after his release, he was gunned down in the street. "I've been expecting it," were his dying words. "The bastards never forget."

🔫 Paul Kelly (1899–1956) Though actor Kelly was only a movie gangster, he managed to obtain genuine criminal credentials by killing a cuckold. For some reason, men were mad for the singularly frumpy Dotty MacKaye. When her husband got wind of her affair with Kelly, he threatened to "kill that son of a bitch Irishman." After a sloppy, drunken fight, hubby lay dead and the actor was on his way to San Quentin. One happy outcome of this sordid affair was the publication of Kelly's goofy love letters from prison, which did much to advance the study of pig latin with the American public. Released from the slammer, Kelly, now really typecast, went back to playing mobsters and film noir creeps—although once, in an ironic departure, he portrayed the warden of San Quentin.

Vincent "Mad Dog" Coll (1909–1932) A baby-faced maniac born in the New York Irish ghetto known as Hell's Kitchen, Coll began his career as a hit man for bootlegger Dutch Schultz, but soon went freelance; in his subsequent war with the Dutchman, gunmen and innocent bystanders—including several children—were mowed down in the streets of Gotham. For a while, Coll kept himself in pocket money by kidnapping for ransom members of other gangs; the underworld, in a rare show of unanimity, put a $50,000 contract on the man they called The "Mad Mick."

Jimmy Burke (Jimmy Conway) (1934–1996) Mafia men are reported to be notoriously stingy tippers, so Burke, who laid $100 on doormen and $500 on bartenders, became known as "Jimmy the Gent." Although he is assumed to have masterminded the Lufthansa heist, the biggest holdup in American history, his fame arose from his peculiar brand of gallantry. He once returned $5,000 some no-good hood had borrowed from his mother, and *then* whacked the son. In *Wiseguy*, author Nicholas Pileggi reported that both the Luccheses and Colombos vied for his services, and "the notion that two Italian-run crime families would even consider having a sit-down to negotiate the services of an Irishman only added to the Burke legend." In the movie *Goodfellas*, Jimmy the Gent was played by Robert De Niro, who is, it should be pointed out, half Irish.

HOLD THAT GRUDGE!

"May none of their race survive,
May God destroy them all,
Each curse of the psalms in the holy books
Of the prophets on them fall. Amen."
— Traditional Irish Curse

The definition of **Irish Alzheimer's:** *You forget everything but the grudges.*

If you wish to pass for Irish, you must realize that while it's your Christian duty to forgive your enemies, you must never, ever, forget their names. The "enemies list" he kept substantiates Richard Nixon's claim to an Irish heritage. And the most Irish thing about John F. Kennedy was his motto, "Don't get mad, get even."

The Kennedys vs. The World

Patriarch Joe Kennedy vowed never to bestow another penny on his alma mater after the Harvard football coach neglected to send Joe Junior off the bench into the 1937 Harvard-Yale game. Matriarch Rose Kennedy disowned her (favorite) daughter Kathleen upon learn-  ing that "Kick" was determined to marry a divorced man, and when Kathleen was killed in a plane crash, refused to attend her funeral, sending instead a memorial mass card—a plea for a soul in purgatory. Attorney General Robert Kennedy hated Jimmy Hoffa so much that he actually had difficulty uttering his name. He marshaled his considerable forces to form the "Get Hoffa Squad," and resorted to some dubiously legal—and quite ineffectual—tactics to nail the Teamsters chief. (Hoffa was himself no slouch in the grudge department. When told JFK had been assassinated, Hoffa gloated, "Now Bobby's just another lawyer.")

Sin vs. High King
Muirchertach MacErca

Back in the sixth century, the high king, married with children, fell for a beautiful girl mysteriously named Sin. (On their first meeting, she pointed out that her name "is not what it seems," explaining that it's actually a synonym for bad weather.) She agreed to become the king's mistress, with the condition that while she was living in the castle, no cleric would be allowed to enter. Sin soon set wife and family packing, and it became evident to all that she was no stranger to the black arts. It took all the efforts of the local bishop to convince the still-smitten king to rid himself of this temptress. When the king confronted Sin with her, well...sin, she informed him that it was all an attempt to avenge her father, whom he had killed in battle. She then set the castle on fire. The king attempted to save himself by jumping in a vat of wine, but drowned instead.

Saint Columbanus vs. Saint Gall

Gall was one of twelve Irish monks who accompanied Columbanus on his mission to save European civilization. In 610, the troublesome Irishmen were thrown out of France and traveled into Italy through the Alps. But Gall decided to remain behind, in Switzerland. He claimed to be unwell, but Columbanus suspected he wanted to stay for the fishing. They quarreled, and before they parted, Columbanus forbade his disciple to ever again say mass. Nevertheless, Gall became popular among the Swiss by means of casting a demon out of

the king's fiancée. (An Alpine monastery and town are named in his honor.) Only on his deathbed did Columbanus relent, sending an emissary with permission for the ancient hermit to resume his priestly duties.

Edward Carson vs. Oscar Wilde

Carson was Wilde's classmate at Trinity College, Dublin, but lagged behind him academically and socially, and often found his frumpiness the subject of Wilde's barbed wit. Carson disapproved of Wilde's glib attitude toward his studies and his flirtation with Roman Catholicism. Twenty years later he got his revenge when he prosecuted Wilde in his libel trial. When Oscar heard that Carson was to be his prosecutor, he sighed, "No doubt he will perform the task with the added bitterness of an old friend." Wilde was right: first Carson (correctly) accused Wilde of lying about his age and then proceeded to mangle some of his verse: "Is that a beautiful phrase?" he asked. "Not as you read it, Mr. Carson," was Wilde's reply.

In his later years, Carson returned to Ireland to oppose Home Rule. He coined the phrase "Ulster will fight, and Ulster will be right!" and formed the Ulster Volunteers, setting in motion a century of aggression and violence.

Free Staters vs. Republicans

For half a century, a feature of Irish political and social life was the ongoing hostility between the treacherous bastards who had accepted the terms of the 1921 Anglo-Irish Treaty and the treacherous bastards who had not.

The Long Grudge began after the Dail (parliament) voted to ratify the treaty. Eamon de Valera (who was, in the opinion of Free State senator Oliver Gogarty, "a cross between a corpse and a cormorant") walked out, and his die-hard Republicans followed. Mick Collins shouted after them, "Deserters! Deserters all to the Irish nation in her hour of trial!" Whereupon Countess Markievicz turned and accused the pro-treaty party of being "Oath breakers and cowards!" Collins howled, "Foreigners! Americans! English!" But the countess had the last word. "Lloyd Georgites!" she shrieked. And she meant it to sting.

Subsequently, an Irish voter's adherence to either of two identical political parties has been based on the memory of who betrayed whose grandfather during the Civil War.

James Joyce vs. The Irish Nation

Ulysses is, among other things, a payback. Jim's former friend and benefactor Oliver Gogarty had somehow offended the sensibilities of Shem the Penman, and in the novel was portrayed as (and is forever remembered only as) the heartless blowhard Buck Mulligan.

The victims of Joyce's grudges included the Irish printer who had censored his book *Dubliners*; the Irish public, which failed to appreciate Ibsen and himself ("And though they spurn me from their door, / My soul shall spurn them evermore"); and Ireland herself, "the old sow that eats her farrow."

In 1948, Nora Barnacle Joyce suggested to the Irish government that her husband's body be returned from Switzerland to Ireland and reburied with a state funeral, an honor that had been bestowed on Yeats. They were decidedly not interested. Years later, when the National Library of Dublin asked her for the original manuscript of *Finnegans Wake*, Nora pointedly informed them that she was sending the manuscript to...the British Museum.

The Joyce Family vs. Samuel Beckett

When Beckett was working in Paris as James Joyce's secretary, he attracted the attention of his idol's daughter, Lucia,

 who was as man-crazy as only a schizophrenic can be. She fell in love with the tall, handsome writer with piercing blue eyes and, really, who could blame her? Beckett, ecstatic to be near Joyce, was not fully aware that he was inadvertently being "paired" with the loopy Lucia, while the Joyces were oblivious to their daughter's worsening mental illness. When Beckett told Lucia he was not romantically interested in her, she was shattered. *La Famille Joyce*, feeling that their daughter had been trifled with, devastated Beckett by banning him from their home.

Years later, the Dubliners-in-exile reconciled after Beckett was stabbed, almost fatally, by a pimp on the streets of Paris. The Joyces, by now aware of how ill their daughter was, paid for Sam's hospital stay and nourished him with Irish home cooking, most notably, custard pudding. In return, he kindly paid a series of visits to Lucia in the asylum.

John Ford vs. The Cast and Crew

John ("call me Sean") Ford was legendary for his directorial genius and for his abuse of actors, whom he caused to endure punches, curses, the odd rock thrown, and swift kicks to the rear. Any actor who rebelled, however mildly, would land in the doghouse—be out of his next film—or sent into permanent exile. Victor McLaglen, Ben Johnson, Harry Carey, and even John Wayne were all banished for years, as was Ford's only son, whose offense was having had the temerity to offer Dad some advice.

Dorothy Kilgallen vs. Frank Sinatra

In her newspaper gossip column, Kilgallen needled the singer endlessly, causing some amateur psychologists to surmise that her animosity sprang from a repressed sexual attraction to him. She was certainly obsessed with his alleged promiscuity—even though her own marriage to radio costar Dick Kollmar was hardly above scrutiny. (Kollmar chased the gals and maybe even the guys. Could you expect anything less from the man who invented the phrase *hubba-hubba*?) Dotty would refer in print to Frank's  suicide attempts, and (slyly) to his walking in on wife Ava and girlfriend Lana *in flagrante*. She even made the unprofessional move of publishing his home address.

Ed Sullivan vs. Jackie Mason

In the early days of television, when Ed Sullivan beat out fellow Irishman Fred Allen for the Sunday evening slot, the embittered Allen observed, "Ed Sullivan will stay on television as long as other people have talent." It is incredible by today's standard of hyperkinetic showbiz energy that a wooden, homely, humorless prig would reign supreme on network TV, but Sullivan did, for over twenty years.

On October 18, 1964, *The Ed Sullivan Show* was interrupted by a presidential address, causing it to run late. In full view of the studio audience, Sullivan feverishly gesticulated to Mason that the comic had two minutes to wrap up his act. Since he was bombing anyway, Mason gestured back at Sullivan and said, "I got fingers for you. You want a finger, here's a finger." After the show, Sullivan screamed, "Who the fuck are you to make fingers at me? I'll make sure you never work in

show business again." The next day, Sullivan wired all the newspapers that Mason's contract was canceled. In the ensuing months, Mason realized he couldn't even get club dates. He tried suing Sullivan for libel, but the suit went nowhere, as—for decades—did Mason's career.

After arterio-sclerosis, an antidote to grudges, had set in, Sullivan ran into the comic at Las Vegas airport. The henna-haired duo embraced while Sullivan gushed, "How *are* you? Why haven't you been on my show lately?"

Mary McCarthy vs. Lillian Hellman

The literary catfight between Mary McCarthy and Lillian Hellman stemmed from a minor political difference the two had about the Spanish Civil War. It has been speculated that the real reason for McCarthy's animosity was a deep-seated resentment over Hellman's greater fame and success. She thought Hellman a lowbrow and found her memoirs a case of shameless and totally dishonest grandstanding—especially the "Julia" segment, in which Hellman portrays herself as a plucky heroine pitted against the Nazis. Still, it came as a surprise when McCarthy used a 1980 Dick Cavett show appearance as an opportunity to rail against Hellman, calling her a "liar" and sputtering, "Every word she writes is a lie, including *and* and *the*."

F. Scott Fitzgerald vs. Ernest Hemingway

Closet Irishman Fitzgerald idolized the macho Hemingway and did much for his career by touting his beefcake prose, believing (wrongly) that Ernest was the better writer. Hemingway thought (rightly) that Fitzgerald was a whiner and a "rummy" with a screwball wife. Fitzgerald best summed up their differences thus: "His inclination is towards megalomania and mine is towards melancholy." In his 1938 short story "The Snows of Kilimanjaro," Hemingway took a brutal and gratuitous swipe at his former patron by name: "Poor Scott Fitzgerald and his romantic awe of the rich." This so wounded Fitzgerald, now down on his luck, that he vowed never to speak to Hemingway again. He planned to snub him at a Hollywood fund-raiser for the Spanish Civil War, but Hemingway, busy playing the dashing Loyalist, never even noticed Fitzgerald not noticing him.

STICK TO YOUR OWN KIND

Like other semioppressed minorities (Canadians, diabetics, gays, Jews), the Irish take a pathetic delight in recognizing their own, and pointing them out. Memorize this list, and murmur—whenever one of the following names comes up—"one of ours, God bless/damn him/her!"

Bet You Didn't Know They Were Irish

Muhammad Ali. The champ is a direct descendant of Abe Grady, from County Clare, who married an emancipated slave in Kentucky.

Admiral John Barry. The "Father of the U.S. Navy" was born in County Wexford.

Boy George. His real name is George O'Dowd and his father is from County Tipperary.

Marlon Brando. According to his autobiography, the actor's family "was mostly of Irish ancestry." At his son's murder trial, the proto-rebel explained his lad's behavior thus: "I come from a long line of Irish drunks."

The Brontës. England's literary sisters were the offspring of Patrick Brunty, an Irish-born clergyman who survived all his children.

Charlie Chaplin. The Little Tramp's mother was Hannah Hill, from Cork.

Kate Chopin. Before her unhappy marriage, the feminist novelist (The Awakening) was Katherine O'Flaherty.

Elvis Costello. Real name: Declan McManus.

Noël Coward. The hypersophisticated British entertainer's grandmother was Mary Kathleen Lynch, from Kerry.

Sir Arthur Conan Doyle. Although he was born in Scotland, the creator of Sherlock Holmes was descended from an old Norman-Irish (Catholic) family.

Isadora Duncan. The avant-garde dancer was raised, in San Francisco, by her Irish-American mother, née O'Gorman. (George Balanchine may have been harboring some anti-Irish bias when he described the aging Isadora as "a drunken fat woman rolling around like a pig.")

Henry Ford. Both of the great industrialist's parents emigrated from Cork; one of his popular car models was named after the street where they lived, Fair Lane.

John Ford. The film director was born Sean O'Feeney, to Irish immigrant parents.

Judy Garland. She always referred to her father, Frank Gumm, as "a charming Irishman."

Greer Garson. Although she was born in County Down, the actress captured the tiny heart of studio head Louis B. Mayer by virtue of her "English beauty and demeanor." But when Garson eloped with the actor who played her son in *Mrs. Miniver*, Mayer decided she was Irish after all.

Mel Gibson. The Australian-American actor is named after Saint Mel, patron of County Longford, where his father was born.

Che Guevara. His father was Ernesto Guevara Lynch, a descendent of immigrants from County Clare. Che died wearing an heirloom from his Irish grandmother Lynch.

Alex Haley. The African-American novelist traced his Roots on his father's side to Ireland—to County Monaghan, no less—where they welcomed him with open arms, until they found out he was a Protestant.

Joel Chandler Harris. The creator of Uncle Remus was born in Georgia, "the son of a wandering Irishman."

Helen Hayes. The great American actress was the niece of singer Catherine Hayes, known as the "Swan of Erin."

Isaac Herzog. The scholar and statesman who became the chief rabbi of Palestine in 1936 had, for the previous decade, been chief rabbi of the Irish Free State.

Alfred Hitchcock. The London-born film director's mother was Emma Whelan, from Cork. The rotund auteur blamed his obsession with food on Emma, whom he once caught sneaking candy out of his Christmas stocking.

"Hulk" Hogan. A full-page spread of the bulky pro wrestler (wearing purple underpants) was featured in *Ireland of the Welcomes* magazine.

Sam Houston. Both he and Davy Crockett were of Scotch-Irish stock, and presumably brought some of the "luck of the Irish" to the Alamo.

Andrew Jackson. Both of Old Hickory's parents came from Carrickfergus, County Antrim.

Henry James. The eminent novelist, and his philosopher brother William, were the grandsons of William James of Bailieborough, County Cavan.

Charles Laughton. On film, he played quintessential Englishmen—Henry VIII and Captain Bligh—but his mother was from Cork. Laughton urged busty young actress Maureen FitzSimons to change her name to O'Hara, surmising that dense Americans would find FitzSimons "too hard to understand."

Lawrence of Arabia. His father's family, the Chapmans, had been Westmeath "landed gentry" since the sixteenth century. Michael Collins invited Lawrence to become commander in chief of the Irish rebel army, much to the horror of Winston Churchill. In a 1932 letter to W. B. Yeats, Lawrence wrote, "I am Irish…It's not my fault, wholly, if I am not more Irish."

C. S. Lewis. The Christian (Anglo-Catholic) theologian and children's writer was born in County Antrim.

Frank Makemie. The founder of American Presbyterianism emigrated from County Donegal.

Guglielmo Marconi. The mother of the Italian-born inventor of radio was Anne Jameson, of the Irish distilling clan.

Edna St. Vincent Millay. The bohemian poet (nicknamed "Leprechaun") was the daughter of Irish American Cora Buzzelle.

Jack Nicholson. His grandfather emigrated from Cork. To his friends, the actor's nickname is "Irish."

Georgia O'Keeffe. Maybe it was the way she dressed but the artist never came across as the typical Gael. Nevertheless, she was: her grandfather Pierce O'Keeffe, was born in Ireland.

Gregory Peck. The film star's mother was born in Dingle, County Kerry.

William Penn. The Quaker leader and founder of Pennsylvania was born in County Cork.

Augustus Saint-Gaudens. The great American monument sculptor was a Dubliner.

Margaret Sanger. The courageous birth-control pioneer was the daughter of Irish immigrants, both fallen-away Catholics.

Lawrence Sterne. The celebrated "English" novelist, author of *Tristram Shandy*, was born in County Tipperary.

John Travolta. His mother was Helen Burke. The film star's interest in Scientology is anomalous, since L. Ron's creed is too left-brained for the Irish in general.

Mark "Marky Mark" Wahlberg. Although the Irish are not noted for posing in their underwear, the model/actor is three-quarters Irish—and from South Boston to boot.

The Duke of Wellington. The British hero of Waterloo was born and raised in County Meath, but always denied being Irish, asserting that "being born in a stable doesn't make you a horse."

Bet You Didn't Know
(and Are Sorry to Hear)
They Were Irish

*The Ancient Order of Hibernians does not publically
proclaim the ethnicity of this crowd.*

Billy the Kid. Born Henry McCarty in New York—or possibly in Ireland—the famous psycho-outlaw, whose first victim was a sheriff named William Brady, was shot to death by a sheriff named Pat Brady.

Dracula. The creator of the immortal blood-sucking count was Dubliner Bram Stoker; some elements of his tale he borrowed from the story "Carmilla" by fellow Dubliner Sheridan Le Fanu, but undead blood drinkers are a feature of Irish folklore. Although married—to Florence Balcombe, a former girlfriend of Oscar Wilde's—Stoker seems, like Wilde, to have been a closet homosexual. He spent his adult life in thrall to the hammy British actor Henry Irving, and went so far as to name his only son after him—thus creating the only Irishman in history called Irving.

Patrick Hitler. When, in the 1930s, young Pat and his mother Bridget Downing Hitler (a Dublin native and the ex-wife of Alois Hitler, Jr.) visited uncle Adolf, the Führer was heard to complain about his "loathsome relatives." Patrick, in turn, leaked to the international press that his family was part Jewish. Patrick eventually served in the U.S. Navy, moved to New York, and changed his last name. But he named his first son Adolf.

Jesse James. The grandfather of the American Robin Hood—or murderous train robber, depending on your point of view—had emigrated from Asdee, County Kerry.

"Lord Haw-Haw." The treacherous Nazi radio propagandist William Joyce was born in Brooklyn, but grew up in Ireland.

"Typhoid Mary" Mallon. The woman who in 1906 introduced the plague to America was an immigrant from Ireland.

President Richard M. Nixon. Upon learning that his great-great-great-great-grandfather Thomas Milhous hailed from Timahoe, County Kildare, Nixon thoughtfully named his dog (an Irish setter) King Timahoe.

President James Polk. The great-grandson of William Polk, an emigrant from County Donegal, America's eleventh president was dismissed by John Quincy Adams as "a man with no wit, no literature, no elegance of language." He was also "rigid, narrow, and obstinate," in the opinion of historian Bernard de Voto. Polk was married to a Calvinist as dour as himself, who banned liquor, card playing, and dancing from the White House. After he stole Texas from Mexico, in America's most naked war of territorial aggression, he died of chronic diarrhea.

General Philip Sheridan. The U.S. Army's Indian-slaughtering "Little Phil" was born (a Catholic) in County Sligo.

President Woodrow Wilson. Ignoring appeals from his Irish-American constituents, the statesman excluded Irish democracy from the ideals for which World War I had made the world safe. Irish nationalist John Devoy called him "the meanest man who ever filled the office of president of the United States." But then, both of Wilson's paternal grandparents were from County Antrim.

Bet You Didn't Know
They Were Not Irish

Appearances and common knowledge to the contrary, Hibernophiles cannot justly lay claim to these celebrities.

The Blessed Virgin Mary. Even though she has been most memorably portrayed on screen by Irish-American actress Linda Darnell in *The Song of Bernadette* (1943), Irish actress Siobhan McKenna in *King of Kings* (1961), Dorothy McGuire in *The Greatest Story Ever Told* (1965), and Irish singer Sinéad O'Connor in *The Butcher Boy* (1998), God's mother was actually Jewish.

Pat Buchanan. In his autobiography, the bellicose reactionary claims that some of his father's people (but not, surely, the Baldwins) were Scotch-Irish. His mother, however, was of pure Teutonic stock.

Tommy Burns. The diminutive heavyweight champ (1906–08) was born Noah Brusso. Likewise, "Mushy" Callahan, welterweight champion (1926–30) was originally Vincent Morris Scheer, and "Tippy" Larkin, junior welterweight champion (1946), was born Antonio Pilleteri.

"Buffalo Bill" Cody. His grandmother Lydia assured the great Plainsman that he was the descendant of Irish kings, but he wasn't. His ancestors hailed from the Channel Islands.

Eamon De Valera. The longtime leader of Ireland (1926–1973) was born in New York City. His father was Spanish.

Arthur Godfrey. Although the popular radio and TV host had freckles, held grudges, and encouraged Carmel Quinn to sing "If you're Irish, come into the parlor," he was the progeny of pure WASP loins.

Katharine Hepburn. Despite the red hair and freckles, her long relationship with Spencer Tracy, and her portrayal of Eugene O'Neill's mother in *Long Day's Journey into Night*, Kate is of the purest Anglo-Saxon stock.

Victor McLaglen. He may have won an Oscar as an IRA traitor in *The Informer*, but he was a Scot—and a Protestant to boot.

Knute Rockne. Although he was played in the movies by Pat O'Brien, the original coach of Notre Dame's "Fighting Irish" football team was a Swede. The University of Notre Dame was founded by a Frenchman and the 1998–99 "Fighting Irish" roster includes a Wizne, a Pettigout, a Denson, and a Rosenthal, but nary an Irish name.

Mickey Rooney. Despite his resemblance to a cruel Thomas Nast cartoon of an Irishman, he is of Scottish descent. And his real name isn't Rooney, either.

Al Smith. The "Happy Warrior" and first Catholic presidential candidate had an Italian father and a German mother.

CHAPTER 8

⚭

HOW TO HAVE YOUR BLADDER NEAR YOUR EYES

OR, HOW THE IRISH SAVED KITSCH

✦ Part Two ✦

Breathe a prayer, drop a tear, good men,
good people. He was the croppy boy.

Like the women and children of the Superior Races (whom they in so many ways resemble) the Celts are not only cute, simple, and illogical, but highly sentimental, "an ardent and impetuous race, easily moved to tears or laughter, to fury or to love," as Thomas Macaulay observed in his *History of England*.

To pass for Irish, you must—regardless of your religious persuasion—learn to weep at the exploits of: brave Father Murphy of the ballad "Boulavogue"; fighting Father Duffy of the "Fighting 69th"; strict-but-fair Father Flanagan of Boys Town; crusading Father Barry of *On the Waterfront*; crooning Father O'Malley of *Going My Way*; and misunderstood Father Dismas Clark, The "Hoodlum Priest."

♛ No matter how stiff your stiff Lace-Curtain Irish upper lip may be, any St. Paddy's Day parade will bring a tear to your eye; likewise you will find a July 12 "Orange" parade tremendously exciting—one way or another.

👄 The eyes of the Stage Irish, when not twinkling, are misty. This latter condition is brought about by the second- or third-hand memory of wrongs inflicted on the innocent Celts, and/or any mention of the word *mother*.

🐚 Sentimentally speaking, the Shanty Irish are the most volatile of all, and given to expressing the spontaneous overflow of powerful emotion by socking a stranger or loved one in the eye.

But the surest way to work any Irish man or woman at all into a frenzy of Irishness is exposure to Irish music.

THE SAME OLD SONG...

Wild I-rish Rose, _____ the sweet-est flow'r that gro

a tempo

The Irish love to sing and dance—although it has never quite been suggested that they have "natural rhythm." In order to pass for Irish, you must on occasion perform or at least visibly appreciate some *real* Irish music—whatever you take that to be.

The ancient Gaels were reportedly most devoted to melodies played on the harp, for which reason that instrument is yet a symbol of the nation; a genuine Irish harp, of the sort played in the castles of the twelfth-century Gaelic-speaking gentry, was a small instrument, played while held against the shoulder. It had a willow-wood frame and strings of brass. We know that professional harpers accompanied poetic recitations, were much respected, frequently blind, and had long fingernails, but, alas, the marvelous melodies they composed are for the most part lost to us. Only two hundred or so songs of the last itinerant harper, Turlough O'Carolan (1670–1738), have sur-vived. They are, of course, exquisite, and today are often employed to add a touch of class to an otherwise rowdy come-all-ye.

♨ Other Irish composers who find favor with the Lace-Curtain crowd include Elizabethan singer and lutist John Dowland, who is often called English although he was born in Dublin; John Field, the Dublin-born pianist-composer who invented the form known as the nocturne; Michael Balfe, violinist, baritone, and composer of *The Bohemian Girl*; Sir Arthur Sullivan, collaborator with lyricist W. S. Gilbert on many excruciatingly clever comic operettas; Sir Hamilton Harty, conductor, whistling virtuoso, and composer of an "Irish" symphony; and prolific Irish-American composer Victor Herbert. In their CD collections one is sure to find performances by classical flutist James Galway.

☙ The Stage Irish prefer the melodies of Ernest R. Ball of Cleveland, Ohio, who wrote the music to "When Irish Eyes are Smiling" and "A Little Bit of Heaven," and had the dubious honor to be portrayed by Dick Haymes in a 1944 film bio. On ceremonial occasions, with a drop taken, they sing along with scratchy recordings by Dublin barroom belters the Wolfe Tones, or scarlet-tressed songbird Carmel Quinn.

🐷 The Shanty Irish, at home and abroad, favor the compositions and vocalizations of Nashville's own Mr. Clint Black.

Victor Herbert (1859–1924) was a cello virtuoso, conductor of the Pittsburgh Symphony Orchestra and the New York Philharmonic, and composer of concertos, a dozen musical comedies, and forty operettas, including *Babes in Toyland* (1903), *The Red Mill* (1906), and *Naughty Marietta* (1910). He was born in Dublin, the nephew of Irish nationalist-novelist Samuel Lover, and although he grew up in Germany and emigrated to the United States at the age of twenty-seven, Herbert remained a fiercely patriotic Irishman. He was president of the fraternal Friendly Sons of St. Patrick and elected, at the 1916 Irish Race Convention in New York, president of the militant Friends of Irish Freedom.

He was the most successful composer for the musical stage of his era—and nobody's fool. Annoyed that he received no royalties when his song hits from *Sweethearts* were played in fancy restaurants, he sued and won, then cofounding (with his friend John Philip Sousa) the American Society of Composers, Authors, and Publishers (ASCAP).

His contracts always specified that "no changes shall be made in the libretto or the music," and that an ice box filled with lager beer be provided in his dressing room.

The Gilded Age
of
Golden Throats

For most "narrowbacks"—that is, second-and third-generation Irish immigrants—"Irish music" meant ballads sung on stage or on record by Irish tenors. And the greatest of these was John McCormack.

Born in 1884 to a working-class family in Athlone, McCormack won the gold medal at the 1903 Irish National Music Festival (defeating another aspiring tenor named James Joyce) and thereafter trained for an operatic career in Italy. He made his American debut in 1909, appearing with opera companies in New York, Boston, and Chicago. In 1914, President Woodrow Wilson requested that McCormack assist the war effort by "helping to keep the flow of sentiment flowing," so he undertook an extensive series of concert tours of America. His programs always included both "art" songs and Irish tunes—traditional ballads as well as Tin Pan Alley hits—and he featured the same repertoire on his many popular recordings.

"The Count," as he preferred to be called once the pope had knighted him, was a commercial and artistic phenomenon, whose only rival was the great Caruso; but for half a century a great many other Irish tenors serenaded—through their noses—the misty-eyed public.

1891. W. J. "Billy" Scanlan, who may have been the original American-Irish tenor, was a veteran of vaudeville and minstrel shows. He got his big break singing "Molly O!" in the Broadway musical *Mavourneen*, but promptly thereafter went mad (of syphilis) and died.

1892. Maggie Cline, vaudeville's first Irish woman comedy singer, nightly brought down the house with her rousing rendition of John W. Kelley's "Throw Him Down, McCloskey," but tenor Charles Marsh had the hit record;

George Gaskin, who was billed as the "Silver-Voiced Irish Tenor," introduced the baseball anthem "Slide, Kelly, Slide."

1895. In his long career, **Dan Quinn** recorded some 2,500 titles, among them "The Sidewalks of New York" (on which he and Mamie O'Rourke tripped the light fantastic).

1897. "Sweet Rosie O'Grady," written and performed by **Maude Nugent**, was a New York City sensation. **Gaskin**'s recording of it topped the charts for fifteen straight weeks.

1898. Chauncey Olcott, born in Buffalo, New York, had made his debut with Lillian Russell in *Pepita*. A master showman, he would star in a series of smash hit musicals, beginning with *A Romance of Athlone*, in which he introduced "My Wild Irish Rose."

1899. Recordings of "My Wild Irish Rose" by both **Gaskin** and **Albert Campbell** topped the charts for two months.

1905. Billy Murray, billed as the "Denver Nightingale," was the first singer to make his reputation solely on recordings rather than on the stage; this year's hit was "My Irish Molly O."

1907. Murray began specializing in "covering" songs by **George M. Cohan**, such as this year's showstopper, "Harrigan."

1910. In *Barry of Ballymore*, **Olcott** introduced "Mother Machree"; **Harry MacDonagh** recorded "Where the River Shannon Flows" and **John McCormack** released recordings of "Come Back to Erin" and "Killarney."

1911. McCormack recorded "Kathleen Mavourneen," as well as his own version of "Mother Machree."

1912. Will Oakland (who was, in fact, a German-born countertenor) had a monster hit with "I'll Take You Home Again, Kathleen."

1913. Charles Harrison released his recording of the Ziegfeld Follies showstopper "Peg O' My Heart."

1914. Olcott introduced "Too-ra-loo-ra-loo-ra, That's an Irish lullaby."

1915. George MacFarlane, a Canadian-born performer of operettas, sang "They Called It Ireland" ("Shure a little bit of Heaven"), and **McCormack** scored with "It's a Long (Long) Way to Tipperary."

1916. In *The Isle o' Dreams*, **Olcott** introduced "When Irish Eyes Are Smiling," and **Charles Harrison**'s record of "Ireland Must Be Heaven, for My Mother Came from There" topped the charts for two months.

1918. Lewis James recorded "The Daughter of Rosie O'Grady."

1920. Harrison released "That Old Irish Mother of Mine" and "Pretty Kitty Kelly."

1921. "Sweet Peggy O'Neil" was a hit for **Billy Jones**, the tenor half of radio's popular Happiness Boys.

1928. McCormack recorded "The Kerry Dance."

"Danny Boy" was the signature tune of Arthur Tracy, an accordionist and tenor billed as the "Street Singer" who was a popular radio performer throughout the 1930s. So was tenor Morton Downey, the "Irish Thrush," who became a favorite of ambassador Joe Kennedy, the husband of glamour-puss Constance Bennett, and father of a gasbag, Morton Downey, Jr.

Tenor Dennis Day (né Eugene McNulty), who was one of comedian Jack Benny's radio sidekicks, made the 1949 hit parade with a novelty number about a belligerent Mick, "Clancy Lowered the Boom."

For years, the favorite tenor of the Irish community in England was Josef Locke (né McLaughlin) a protégé of John McCormack. The droll saga of Locke's escape from the clutches of British tax collectors is told in the 1991 film *Hear My Song*, in which Ned Beatty plays Locke, lip-synching to the singing of Frank Patterson, who is Ireland's reigning tenor.

Meanwhile, in America, a baritone had captured the green flag.

Der Bingle

Bing Crosby was one of the first singers to take advantage of the newly invented microphone, virtually inventing the intimate style that came to be known as crooning. (Bandleader Tommy Dorsey advised the young Sinatra to listen to Crosby. "All that matters to him is the words, and that's all that should matter to you, too.")

Bing was Irish only on his mother's (Catherine Harrigan's) side, but he was unquestionably, ostentatiously a Roman Catholic, which was good enough for Irish-American music lovers, who in 1942 bought a million copies of his recording of "Adeste Fideles"—sung in Latin, yet.

He had a pleasant voice, and a true one. Not only could he croon, he could swing. Of his 2,600 recordings, dozens became million-sellers, and his version of "White Christmas" remains the best-selling record of all time.

But, most mysteriously, Crosby also became a leading man in the movies, the box-office champ from 1944 to 1948—despite his peculiar looks and failed attempts to pin back his jug ears with spirit gum.

In justice, it must be said that Der Bingle didn't become aggressively Irish until 1944, when he won an Academy Award as Father O'Malley in *Going My Way*, and had a million-selling record with "Too-ra-loo-ra-loo-ra." In '45, he reprised the O'Malley role in *The Bells of St. Mary's*. In 1948, his version of the ultra-Irish "Galway Bay" (a song that had been written in 1927 by a British neurologist) spent seventeen weeks on the hit parade. He proceeded to costar with Barry Fitzgerald in the astonishingly kitschy film *Top o' the Morning* (1949) and to release a series of ghastly Stage Irish "novelty" records: "Christmas in Killarney," "My Girl's an Irish Girl," "An Irishman's Idea of Love," "Two-Shillelagh O'Sullivan," etc.

In America, the Irish are inevitably replaced by Italians: in the 1920s, Al Capone took over Chicago's underworld from Deanie O'Banion; in the 1930s, Fiorello La Guardia replaced Jimmy Walker as New York's mayor; and in the late 1940s Sinatra eclipsed Crosby as the nation's most popular pop singer. (So In did Italian become and so Out was Irish that Kentucky-Irish Rosemary Clooney, the most popular female vocalist of the fifties, achieved nationwide stardom by passing for Italian with her first big hit, "Come on-a My House."

Yet the older Irish crooner continued to torment the Italian Sinatra. In a famous 1962 incident, JFK snubbed Sinatra to stay, instead, at Bing's house. Even during Sinatra's papal audience, the pope kept asking Frank about Bing—perhaps because at the time Crosby had been busy making hit records out of such Catholic hymns as "Faith of Our Fathers."

Kiss My Londonderry Air

Possibly the most popular—nay, inevitable—of Irish songs is "Danny Boy." Its lyric was composed by one Frederick E. Weatherly, in 1913, but the melody first appeared in print, untitled, in the 1855 *Petrie Collection of the Ancient Music of Ireland*. A maiden lady, Jane Ross, from the County of Londonderry (sic), had submitted the "aire" to Petrie, accompanied by a note saying it was "very old." Around Derry it was believed that the melody was learned from the fairies. Petrie assured his readers that despite its Ulster origins, the tune is "distinctly Irish," observing that in Londonderry, "the old Irish race still forms a great majority of its peasant inhabitants."

It is a peculiar ballad: a boy must go (to war?) and leave the heartbroken singer behind; he is petitioned to return and say a prayer over the singer's grave. Although it appears to be a lover's—or a mother's—lament, it is invariably performed by a male.

"Danny Boy" stayed popular throughout the twentieth century, in recorded versions by such luminaries as Count Basie, Ray Price, Frank Sinatra, and Bing Crosby, as well as a roster of operatic talent. It is the party piece in the repertoire of every amateur Irish tenor, a St. Patrick's Day staple, and a favorite at weddings and wakes, always guaranteed to bring a tear to the eye. The tune reached a nadir of sorts when for seven years it served as the theme for the treacly TV series *The Danny Thomas Show*.

Just Folks

In Ireland, throughout the 1950s, classically trained and jazz-influenced composer Seán Ó Riada was rediscovering and transforming the ancient Irish airs—his major work is his magnificent score to the 1960 film *Mise Eire*. But it was not until a Sunday evening in 1961 that Irish music of the non–Tin Pan Alley sort was heard in North America, when onto the stage of *The Ed Sullivan Show* bounded the three Clancy Brothers from Tipperary and Tommy Makem from Armagh, all clad in cable-knit Aran sweaters and belting out "Brennan on the Moor."

As charter members of the 1960s "folk scare" the Clancys influenced everyone from Bob Dylan in Greenwich Village to Paddy Moloney back in Dublin; the former began setting new words to Irish folk tunes, and the latter formed the Chieftains, who eventually rose to fame by providing the soundtrack to the 1975 movie *Barry Lyndon*.

Today, individuals of the Stage Irish class enjoy partaking in one-upmanship debates as to whether the Chieftains—or Altan, Clannad, the Bothy Band, De Danaan, Planxty, or any other modern makers of Irish music—are "folk" or "trad." A simple rule of thumb: if a guitar is employed and/or the performer's name is pronounceable, it's folk.

Trad instruments include uillean bagpipes, a late-eighteenth-century adaptation of the ancient Scots instrument, but played with bellows; the wooden flute, or tin penny whistle (both likewise eighteenth-century imports to Ireland); the bodhrán, a drum that resembles a large tambourine and is played with sticks (the name means "deafener"); a fiddle, which is a violin played with the musician's left hand kept in the first position; and (sometimes) a button accordion or a concertina.

The Greatest Moments of Irish Rock

Them (with **Van Morrison**), *Them*, 1965

Van Morrison, *Moondance*, 1970

Gilbert O'Sullivan, *Himself*, 1972

Thin Lizzy, *Thin Lizzy*, 1971

Horslips, *The Tain*, 1974

Rory Gallagher, *Irish Tour*, 1974

Planxty, *The Planxty Collection*, 1976

Elvis Costello (Declan McManus), *My Aim Is True*, 1977

The Boomtown Rats, *Ratrospective*, 1983

The Pogues, *Rum, Sodomy & the Lash*, 1985

U2, *The Joshua Tree*, 1987

Enya (Eithne Ni Bhraonain), *Watermark*, 1988

The Waterboys, *Fisherman's Blues*, 1988

The Hothouse Flowers, *People*, 1988

Van Morrison & the Chieftains, *Irish Heartbeat*, 1988

The Cranberries, *Everybody Else Is Doing It So Why Can't We*, 1993

Sinéad O'Connor, *I Do Not Want What I Haven't Got*, 1990

The canon of the traditional Irish tunes (never say "songs") that these musicians play was collected, preserved, and published in 1907 by Francis O'Neill, an amateur flute player and Chicago's chief of police.

An outdoor festival featuring Irish pop, folk, and trad music is known as a *fleadh*, pronounced "flah." In Gaelic, it means "orgy"—but don't let that fool you.

The Playboy (of the Western World) All-Star Jazz Band

Horns: Bunny Berigan, Maynard Ferguson
Cornet: Bobby Hackett
Guitar: Eddie Condon
Clarinet: Jimmy Dorsey
Trombone: Tommy Dorsey
Saxophone: Gerry Mulligan
Drums: Mickey Hart
Piano: Hoagy Carmichael
Vocals: Helen O'Connell, Anita O'Day, Bing Crosby

...AND DANCE

In North America today, fifty thousand people—most of them teenage girls—are being taught "traditional Irish dancing" by certified, qualified teachers of the art (who are more numerous than in Ireland itself).

Many of these facially expressionless, flamboyantly costumed high-steppers hope eventually to compete in the annual World Irish Dancing Championship, an eight-day *céilidh* held in Cork each Easter, in which 2,500 dancers from Australia, Canada, England, New Zealand, Scotland, the USA— even Ireland—participate.

Irish dance—the "Irish jig" —is certainly distinctive. To music in 6/8 time, the dancer's feet execute a prescribed pattern of steps with great and increasing rapidity, while the upper body is held absolutely rigid. But the question arises as to how "traditionally" Irish this style of dancing is.

Jiggers

The jig is an ancient Scottish–Northern English folk dance that had a brief vogue in the court of Queen Elizabeth I. Thence it migrated to France, where it became known as a *gigue*, and was all the rage among the courtiers of Louis XIV. Not until the early eighteenth century was it introduced to Ireland, by traveling (French) "dancing masters."

The Irish, peasants and gentry alike, became keen students and practitioners, not only of solo jigs, but also of the more Scottish reels and French *contre* dances. Here, in part, is a Gaelic poem of 1725 (in Dean Jonathan Swift's translation):

> *They dance in a Round*
> *Cutting capers and Ramping,*
> *A Mercy the Ground*
> *Did not burst with their stamping.*
> *The Floor is all wet*
> *With Leaps and with Jumps,*
> *While the Water and Sweat*
> *Splish splash in their Pumps.*

Despite the Penal Laws, through rebellions and repressions, the Irish danced. Until the potato crop failed, and the dancing stopped.

Postfamine, the newly, grimly puritanical Catholic clergy (see "A Brief History of Irish-American Sex") took a dim view of dancing, for it was an activity in which they had reason to believe the participants took pleasure. Priests not only preached against it, they also patrolled by night the rural areas where it sometimes occurred, armed with sin-smiting blackthorn sticks. Thus, "a whole local culture revolving around crossroads dances and itinerant dance-masters was practically wiped out" (Anthony Bluett, *Things Irish*).

Traditional Irish dancing managed to survive only in North America, where, among the Scotch-Irish of the Appalachians, set dances became square dances, and solo jigging evolved into "buck" dancing.

Meanwhile, back in Ireland, the twentieth century loomed, bringing with it the phonograph and the radio. The native clergy gasped to behold the chaste youth of Ireland indulging in the fox-trot—dancing belly to belly, leaving no room between them whatever for the Holy Ghost. What choice had they then, but to make compulsory the dancing of the formerly prohibited jigs and reels?

In this crusade, they made common cause with the recently founded Gaelic League, a semipolitical, somewhat racist organization whose mission was to revive, or failing that, to invent Gaelic traditions. In 1899, the first national Festival of Irish Culture (*ardh feis*) featured incomprehensible recitations, plenty of tweed, ersatz kilts, modified bagpipes borrowed from the Scots, and exhibitions of vigorous, neutered jigging.

After independence, the government introduced Irish dancing into the curriculum of National Schools—as a competitive sport. "They believe that Satan with all his guile is baffled

by a four-hand reel and cannot make head or tail of the Rakes of Mallow. I do not think that there is any real ground for regarding Irish dancing as a sovereign spiritual or national prophylactic. If there is, heaven help the defenceless nations of other lands," observed Flann O'Brien, that well-known refuser of the festivities.

And then, along came *Riverdance*. Originally, it was a mere seven-minute routine, the Irish entry in the 1993 Eurovision Song Contest, created to showcase the step-dancing talent of Michael Flatley (the first American-born winner of the All-World Championship), with music by ex-Planxty member Bill Whelan.

Ireland won the contest, a video of *Riverdance* became an international hit, and the producer (Moyra Doherty of

Donegal) resolved to expand her wee creation into a mighty stage spectacle, which opened in Dublin in February 1995. A video of this version—featuring the leaping, shirtless Flatley partnering the long-stemmed (and likewise American-born) Jean Butler—is the one American PBS viewers apparently can't get enough of.

The show moved to London in June, and within a year (but without Flatley) to Radio City in New York for St. Patrick's Day, 1996. Three road-show versions currently tour the planet, in competition with Flatley's own modestly titled spin-off, *Lord of the Dance.*

What *is* it about *Riverdance?* After all, Whelan's score (which won a Grammy) is, at best, a load of New Age syntho-Celt. The electronically enhanced, ruthlessly synchronized stomping of the chorus puts one in mind of a speeded-up film of invading storm troopers. The folk-dancers-of–the-world intervals are simply cringe-inducing.

Author Frank McCourt has written that, for him, Irish step dancing (which as a child in Limerick he had learned to despise) was redeemed in the moment Jean Butler *raised her hands above her waist*, smiled, and *touched her hair.*

Maybe the reason for *Riverdance*'s astonishing success is that it reconnected, after 150 years, Irish dancing with excitement, glamour, passion, even—keep your voice down, now, the children might be listening—sex.

Hoofers

While regimented, competitive Celtic jigging was a feature of the countless *ceilís* organized and staged by the Gaelic League in Ireland and North America, creative, expressive "Irish dancing" took to the stage and screen.

Although there had been other Irish-American "song-and-dance men" before him—blackface minstrel Dan Bryant, soft shoe dancer Pat Rooney, and tapper Eddie Foy, Sr.—**George M. Cohan** became, and remains, the archetype. Writing, composing, and usually starring in several Broadway musicals a year from 1901 to 1928, he zealously emphasized the "American" in "Irish American," waving the "Grand Old Flag" as "George Washington Jr." and "That Yankee Doodle Boy." Author, showman, son of famine immigrants, and entrepreneur, George M. was also something of a little shit—a prig, a union buster, a martinet, and an egomaniac. He gave permission for a 1942 film bio—in which Jimmy Cagney was to star—on condition that there be no 'love scenes' included. He meant boy-girl stuff, of course. His life was a one-man love story.

Oliver Goldsmith could have been thinking of Cohan some 150 years earlier when he wrote, "On the stage he was natural, simple, affecting. 'Twas only when he was off he was acting."

George Murphy was a mushy-faced singer and dancer in movie musicals who never got the girl (unless the girl was Shirley Temple). He would have sunk into obscurity except that, incredibly, he was elected to the U.S. Senate in 1964, beginning the phenomenon of unqualified hams entering government. He used his seat as a forum for his reactionary politics and to catapult Ronald Reagan to power. Murphy's

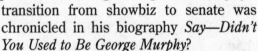

transition from showbiz to senate was chronicled in his biography *Say—Didn't You Used to Be George Murphy?*

Lanky, open-faced **Dan Dailey** began as a serious actor before blossoming into a popular song-and-dance man in postwar movies, until rumors began circulating Hollywood about his cross-dressing. *Confidential* even published an article with pictures, "Dan Dailey in Drag." Fashion choices aside, after filming *There's No Business Like Show Business*, in which Donald O'Connor played his son, Dailey ran off with O'Connor's wife.

Donald O'Connor, like fellow Irishmen Cohan and Buster Keaton, spent his childhood as a prop in his parents' vaudeville routine. In those freewheeling days before child protection agencies, the youngsters were tossed around the stage and bounced off the floor as part of the act. Though O'Connor never took dancing lessons, he became the goofy guy with an altar-boy face in Hollywood musicals, combining song, dance, and acrobatics. He starred in a series of "Francis the Talking Mule" movies until he realized the mule was getting more fan mail, then achieved the lowest-rated television show in history. Ironically, his one straight role was playing Buster Keaton, in the biopic of his life.

Ray Bolger started in vaudeville. His classic turns included the lead in *Where's Charley?* (1952) and the Scarecrow in 1939's *The Wizard of Oz*. What he didn't realize was that his character makeup from *Wizard* would leave his mouth and chin permanently scarred, so that he resembled the Scarecrow for the rest of his life. (Interestingly, *The Wizard of Oz* is almost an all-Irish production, as befits a movie about an Emerald City: Besides Bolger, Judy Garland, Frank Morgan (the Wizard), Jack Haley (the Tin Man), Billie Burke (the Good Witch), special-effects supervisor Buddy Gillespie, and director Victor Fleming were all Micks. Even the head winged monkey was played by Pat Walshe, an Irishman. In later years, the Scarecrow Bolger and the Tin Man Haley would nod to each other every Sunday at mass in the Church of the Good Shepherd in Beverly Hills.

Gene Kelly, actor-director-dancer-choreographer-singer, started as a chorus boy on Broadway, where he developed his dance technique, a hybrid of ballet and tap. He elbowed out both Dailey and Murphy for his first movie role, and went on to be the macho counterpoint to Fred Astaire in Hollywood. Indeed, it was Astaire who called Kelly his "favorite dancing partner" and complimented his voice, that "whiskey Irish tenor." With his work on *Singin' in the Rain* and *An American in Paris*, Kelly did nothing less than reinvent the Hollywood musical.

CHAPTER 9

HOW TO VOTE IRISH

PADDY LEONARD
What am I to do about my rates and taxes?
BLOOM
Pay them my friend.
PADDY LEONARD
Thank you.

The year was 1970. While left-wing Irish-American Jesuit priest Daniel Berrigan was picketing Nixon's White House, right-wing Irish-American Jesuit priest John McLaughlin was inside, advising the president. Thus it may be seen that individual Irish folk—including you—may hold a range of political positions; pacifist, nationalist, Fascist, liberal, reactionary, Socialist, even moderate.

Nevertheless, it may fairly be said that the Irish, at home and abroad, are inclined to be (small *c* or large) conservatives. This is one reason that, in America, they have traditionally voted Democrat.

Eire itself has, since independence, been ruled by either the Fine Gael or the Fianna Fáil parties, both of which, to the casual observer, appear indistinguishably right-of-center. "We were the most conservative revolutionaries in history," wrote Kevin O'Higgins, Free State Minister for Home Affairs and Justice. During subsequent election campaigns, the leaders of these parties have consistently accused each other of being *insufficiently* conservative. Long-time Fianna Fáil leader Eamon De Valera recognized Roman Catholicism as Ireland's state religion, banned divorce and contraception, and wrote a note of condolence upon the occasion of Hitler's death. Yet when Dev first came to power, in 1932, his FineGael opposition maintained he was "proceeding along the Bolshevik path almost as precisely as if he was getting his orders from Moscow."

🎩 Lace-Curtain Left

In his essay "The Soul of Man Under Socialism," Oscar Wilde passionately endorsed the coming red revolution, for which his fellow Dubliner George Bernard Shaw was a lifelong propagandist. (When G.B.S. circulated a petition on behalf of the anarchists condemned to death in the Chicago Haymarket Riot, Wilde was the only other man of letters in London to sign it.) The present Irish Communist Party was

founded by Cecil Day-Lewis, poet, scholar, and father of actor Daniel; today, Ireland's outstanding parlor pink is diplomat, scholar, and gasbag Dr. Conor Cruise O'Brien.

Helen Gahagan Douglas, a California liberal-intellectual, was smeared as "pink" by young Richard Nixon, who thus destroyed her career and jump-started his own. What remains of the American Left establishment (now that author Michael Harrington, House Speaker "Tip" O'Neill, progressive attorney Paul O'Dwyer, and Justice William F. Brennan are gone) is led by Irish-American senators named Kerrey, Kennedy, Leahy, and Moynihan.

🎩 Stage Left

Although Lenin approved—after the fact—of the Easter Rebellion, the real Ireland–Moscow nexus in the thirties consisted entirely of novelist Peadar O'Donnell and agitator "Pa" Murray. The latter once visited Moscow, seeking weapons for the IRA. Lenin asked him, "How many bishops did you hang?" "None," replied Murray. "Ah," said Lenin, "you people are not serious at all.")

Ireland's oldest political party—founded "to establish a workers' republic" by Easter 1916 martyr James Connolly and James Larkin—is Labour. From time to time, these peaceful Socialists have had a small share of power in the Irish government, much to the scandal of the American Irish. (In 1960, *The Tablet*, the newspaper of the Brooklyn diocese, noted with alarm "an Ireland subject to the seductive siren call of the Left and the domination of an alien and atheistic ideology.") Slum-born Irish dramatists Sean O'Casey and Brendan Behan claimed to be unreconstructed Communists.

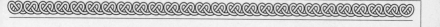

LEFT...

🐷 Shanty Left

The cause of Ireland's working class was espoused by labor leaders Larkin and Connolly, and by novelist (*The Informer*) Liam O'Flaherty.

This side of the Atlantic, defenders of the proletariat have included Irish-American "Big Bill" Haywood, a founder of the Industrial Workers of the World. Found guilty of sedition in 1918, he fled to Russia—where he proclaimed that he had no intention of becoming a Communist, since he "knew how to sock scabs and policemen" but he wasn't "long on the ideological stuff." He is buried in the Kremlin, as is Elizabeth Gurley Flynn, the "Rebel Girl" who once chaired the Communist Party of America. Other red menaces with a touch of the green include Cork-born labor organizer Mother Jones, Trotskyite Chicago novelist James T. Farrell, New York Transport Workers Union (TWUA) leader Mike Quill, New Deal priest John Ryan, labor leader George Meany, and former Chicago Seven defendant turned politician Tom Hayden, who has recently announced his return to his Celtic roots.

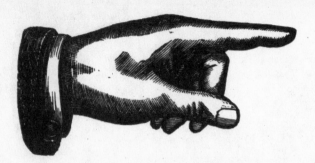

and/or RIGHT

🎩 Stage Right

The most flamboyant of the native Irish right-wingers was a former IRA officer and admirer of Mussolini, Eoin O'Duffy, who, in the early 1930s, commanded a small, goose-stepping army of Blue Shirts. More recently, the

Fianna Fáil *taoiseach* (prime minister) Charles Haughey, or "Great National Bastard" as he was affectionately known, was not above red-baiting when campaigning against a Labour opponent. A populist who lived like a king, a stern moralist with a dowdy wife and a well-known mistress, an outspoken law-and-order advocate who tapped phones and ran guns, his reign collapsed in a flurry of financial scandals.

American superpatriots still love to sing "You're a Grand Old Flag," by Stage Irish union-busting song-and-dance man George M. Cohan. The popular "Radio Priest," Father Charles Coughlin, was a crypto-Nazi, who once called President Herbert Hoover "the Holy Ghost of the Rich," thus adding blasphemy to his list of sins. TV emcee Ed Sullivan was a tireless exposer of showbiz pinkos in his newspaper column.

But the poster boy of the Stage Irish–American Right is Ronald Reagan, who, in his longest-running role, portrayed the commander in chief of the United States for eight years. It is not surprising that Reagan defected from the Democrats. His immigrant Irish ancestors had already changed their religion and the spelling of the family name. Ronnie handed over the day-to-day running of the country to his benefactors, the owner-operators of the military-industrial complex, and devoted himself to taking plenty of naps.

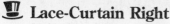

🎩 Lace-Curtain Right

In the 1930s, William Butler Yeats, who aspired in all things to be aristocratic, dabbled in extreme-right politics, going so far as to compose a few martial ditties for Ireland's small and silly Fascist Party.

Today's American ultraconservatives include high-falutin' Irish-American pundits William F. Buckley, Jr., and R. Emmett Tyrell; many of their projects are funded by remnants of the plutocratic Irish-American Mellon clan.

Head House Speaker Tip O'Neal played out the conflict of two classic Irish archetypes: the dedicated schoolmaster (O'Neill) and the town gobshite (Reagan). "He only works three hours a day," lamented Tip. "It's sinful that this man is president of the United States."

🐷 Shanty Right

The "Plain People of Ireland" to whom Dev often addressed his thoughts were for the most part small farmers and devout Roman Catholics—members of the Irish Christian Front, the Knights of Columbus, the Holy Name Society, and the Legion of Mary. In election after election, they endorsed the government's strict censorship of films and books, and bans against both divorce and the importation or sale of contraceptives (which lasted from 1935 to 1985). The (equally Plain) protestant Irish of the North are equally sectarian/reactionary—their elected representatives to Westminster are usually to be found to the right of the Tories, while in Belfast the Reverend Ian Paisley has declared that "the Roman Catholic Church is getting nearer to communism every day."

In America, lumpen-conservatives are distinguished by their fear of "minorities" and hatred of red Russian Communists. *How the Irish Became White*, by historian Noel Ignatiev, describes in excruciating detail the virulent self-serving racism of the entire American-Irish working class. When it comes to anticommunism, Senator Joe McCarthy remains the epitome of Shanty Irish bluster; yet we may cherish as well the words of Mike Hammer, alter ego of enormously popular Irish-American author Mickey Spillane: "I killed more people tonight than I have fingers on my hands. I shot them in cold blood and enjoyed every minute of it. They were Commies…red sons of bitches."

EARLY and/or OFTEN

The Democratic Party was one of the few American institutions in which nineteenth-century Irish immigrants felt welcome; as early as 1804, the Irish in New York City and Philadelphia were instrumental in Jefferson's defeat of Adams and the anti-immigrant Federalist Party.

In 1832, the Irish enthusiastically supported Andy Jackson—one of their own—and by the time of the (prefamine) elections of 1844, they had already become "Yellow Dog Democrat." That year, 95 percent of them voted Polk and the straight Democratic ticket.

The struggling Irish working class opposed emancipation, fearing the competition for jobs by African Americans. Lincoln's antislavery stance confirmed their anti-GOPism to such an extent that in 1884, despite strong support for Republican presidential candidate James G. Blaine by exiled patriots John Devoy and Patrick Ford in the *Irish World*, a majority of the American Irish voted for Democrat Grover Cleveland, out of pure begrudgery.

In 1928, they rallied behind the doomed presidential campaign of the somewhat Irish Al Smith, but not until John F. Kennedy's run in '59 did they again take any real interest in federal politics. They had made an important discovery—that, in the words of statesman "Tip" O'Neill, "All politics is local."

"For the Irish, politics was a functioning system of power and not an exercise in moral judgment. While Henry Adams despaired of the American experience, the Irish took over City Hall," wrote William V. Shannon in *The American Irish*.

Boston mayor Theodore Lyman reassured the Brahmins, even as the famine Irish began pouring into their city, that "the Irish are a race that will never be infused with our own, but will always remain distinct and hostile."

The "distinct and hostile" immigrants—a quarter million of them—committed themselves into the care of ward bosses such as Matthew Keany in the North End or Martin Lomasney, a lantern-jawed stogie chewer known as "the Mahatma," in the West End. The bosses would find them jobs and/or housing. The new arrivals, in return, registered as Democrats.

By 1880, an East End saloon keeper named P. J. Kennedy had taken over Boston's Democratic "machine," and a few years later Hugh O'Brien was elected mayor. In 1905—by which time the Hub was fully half-Irish—P. J.'s hated rival, the North Ender John Francis "Honey Fitz" Fitzgerald, took over City Hall. The bosses made their peace; in 1914, Kennedy's son Joe married Fitzgerald's daughter Rose.

That very year, the magnificent James Michael Curley won the mayoralty, which office he held—except for brief periods in the governor's mansion and a federal penitentiary—until 1950.

In **New York City**, the Irish become a force in municipal politics in 1870, when a first-generation Irish prosecutor named Charles O'Conor brought down the Tweed Ring, and "Honest John" Kelly took over Tammany Hall. With Tammany's backing, William R. Grace (born in Cork) was elected the Empire City's first Irish Catholic mayor, in 1880. The city's Democratic machine was assembled by canny businessman, alleged racketeer and liberal reformer "Big Tim" Sullivan (1863–1913), and efficiently operated by former saloon keeper George Murphy. Nor did Irish hegemony in the politics of the Big Apple end with the 1932 downfall of Jimmy Walker, the dapper, wise-cracking, high-living "Night Mayor." From 1946 to 1950, the Apple's mayor was Mayo-born William O'Dwyer.

The Irish arrived in **Chicago** in 1838, to dig canals and build railroads. They were first recognized as a political force in 1855, when the ruling Know-Nothing party outlawed beer and the Irish joined with their sometime rivals the Germans in staging the "Lager Beer Riots" before voting the bastards out.

The Irish-friendly if fabulously corrupt administrations of mayors Carter Harrison and Carter Harrison II depended upon the support of a picturesque pair of First Ward aldermen, the voluminous "Bath-House" John Coughlin, born "bare arse poor from Roscommon," and the diminutive Michael "Hinky Dink" McKenna from Limerick.

Chicago's Democratic machine was created by Roger "the Gas Man" Sullivan; Edward J. Kelly was the first mayor of their own elected by South Side (Irish) Democrats. Three more followed, between 1933 and 1976, the most (in)famous of them being Richard Daley, who ruled the Windy City from 1955 to 1976.

By 1870, the population of **San Francisco** was one-third Irish. Although the city's Democratic machine had been created, in 1851, by first-generation immigrant David Broderick, Mick-bashing "Committees of Vigilance" kept the Irish in their place until the mayoralty of Patrick McCarthy in 1909.

CHAPTER 10

☙

A BRIEF HISTORY OF IRISH SEX

he touched me Father and what harm if he did
where and I said on the canal bank like a fool

What's the definition of Irish foreplay? "Brace yourself, Bridget!" goes the old joke. Not long ago, some wag made a fortune publishing a coffee-table book entitled *Irish Erotic Art*. Its pages were blank. Get it?

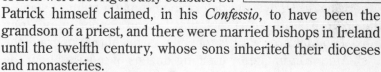

It is customary to blame the notorious prudery of the Irish on the influence of their Catholic-fundamentalist clergy. But the populations of other, equally Roman Catholic nations are not famously chaste. Take France, which shuts down every August 15 in honor of the Blessed Virgin Mary, but gave the world pasties, the bidet, and Brigitte Bardot.

Furthermore, the original pastors of Erin were not rigorously celibate: St. Patrick himself claimed, in his *Confessio*, to have been the grandson of a priest, and there were married bishops in Ireland until the twelfth century, whose sons inherited their dioceses and monasteries.

The moral theology of the Irish clergy—and thus the sexual mores of the Irish laity—took a turn for the psychotically ascetic only after 1695, when Britain's Penal Laws closed all the Catholic seminaries. For a century thereafter, aspiring Irish priests, in order to pursue their vocations, studied in France—where, since 1640, the grimly puritanical heresy of Jansenism had dominated theological thought.

When the Penal Laws began to be repealed, the Irish seminary of Maynooth opened in 1795 and the restored-to-power Irish clerical hierarchy was made up exclusively of leftover killjoy Jansenists, who were soon joined in their sex-negative labors by "missionary" priests from Victorian England.

So now the church absolutely forbade any and all premarital sex, while the state had already made marriage itself economically impossible—for an Irishman could neither own land nor get a decent job. Thus, by the combined imperial efforts of Rome and London, coitus among the natives was virtually eliminated.

Even among the married, the Irish clergy encouraged a no-nooky state of affairs known as "Josephite" in honor of the long-suffering husband of Blessed Mary Ever Virgin.

Nevertheless, the Irish were, as an immigrant underclass, stereotyped in America as sex fiends, bestially promiscuous—as evidenced by their shocking fecundity. A number of young Shanty Irish women were even alleged to be prostitutes! The myth of the randy Gael endured. In 1933, Judge John M. Woolsey admitted James Joyce's "obscene" novel *Ulysses* to the USA on the grounds that, while "the theme of sex" is "recurrent"…"it must be remembered that his locale was Celtic."

Then, as war clouds gathered over Europe, a cabal of Irish Americans in Hollywood determined to put a cultural spin on the proverb "England's problem is Ireland's opportunity." John Ford, Leo McCarey *et al.* launched a media blitz to upgrade the Irish-American image by creating dozens of movies about the Irish as a lot of feisty but sentimental celibates—be they priests, cops, crooks, hoofers, athletes, or patriots.

By VJ Day, the American public had been brainwashed, convinced of the absolute, inborn chastity of everyone remotely Irish—including the handsome returned war hero, John F. Kennedy.

Thus it may be seen that the ongoing Irish-American reputation for chastity and/or prudery is a triumph of "spin"—a public relations job. We recommend a similar strategy to our allegedly oversexed African-American and Hispanic-American fellow citizens.

THE IRISH: UNLUCKY IN LOVE
🐾 Part One 🐾

Ireland is proverbially "the land of happy wars and sad love songs." From the ancient mythic tales (*"Deirdre of the Sorrows"*) to Tin Pan Alley ballads ("Come Back to Erin, Mavourneen") to contemporary films (*The Crying Game*) Irish love stories tend to feature treachery, and end in heartbreak. Some star-crossed all-Irish couples:

Tristan and Isolde. Okay, so she was an Irish princess, while he was merely Celtic (Welsh). But their tragic love story is immortal. Wagner, among others, tells the messy tale of their forbidden adulterous passion and mutual suicide.

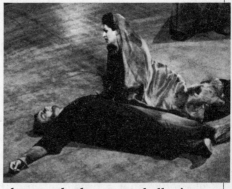

Dermot and Gráinne. Finn McCool was the leader of Ireland's mythic defenders, the Fianna; his handsome nephew ran away with his beautiful wife. (Gráinne fell in love with Dermot once she saw the love spot, *ball-seirce*, in the center of his forehead.) Finn pursued them; they ended up dead.

President Andrew Jackson and Rachel (née Donelson) Robards Jackson. Old Hickory (both of whose parents were Irish immigrants) fought two duels defending his wife's honor; she died, it is said, as a result of the campaign of slander against her.

Robert Emmet and Sarah Curran. Her prominent father disowned her for abetting his revolutionary plans; she waved a tearful farewell to her true love as he mounted the scaffold.

William Butler Yeats and Maud Gonne. The arch-poet's lifelong Muse constantly refused him; he eventually proposed to her daughter, who did likewise.

Oscar and Constance Lloyd Wilde. She endured her husband's flirtations with actresses and his tendency to blather about their private life; e.g. "One should always be in love. That is the reason one should never marry." She even agreed to dress in unflattering garb for Oscar's theme dinner parties. But his obsession with the snotty, treacherous Lord Alfred Douglas eventually proved too much for even this most long-suffering of Irish wives.

Leopold and Molly Bloom. She is an unfaithful Penelope, he a self-abusing Ulysses.

Barbara Stanwyck and Frank Fay. The marriage of these two icons of Irish Hollywood inspired the film *A Star Is Born*. Incredibly, the swaggering, tough-talking Babs was physically abused by the drunken, over-the-hill vaudevillian with whistling false teeth. Understandably, her next husband was the effete Robert Taylor.

John F. Kennedy and Gene Tierney. While the glamorous movie star was still married to Oleg Cassini, she and the young would-be congressman had an intense, yearlong affair. But her very Lace-Curtain (Republican, Episcopalian) family found the Kennedy crowd "common."

Eunice Kennedy and Joe McCarthy. The sister of the allegedly liberal president and the right-wing nut dated, but never made it to the altar.

Grace Kelly and Bing Crosby. Despite her ice-maiden on-screen image, Grace was notorious for having (in the words of Bette Davis) "round heels." Her affair with Crosby began while his wife lay dying; eventually, he proposed—but by then, Grace's prince had come.

Marlon Brando and Anna Kashfi. Ever the renegade, Brando married the exotic Indian actress only to discover that she was really Joan O' Callaghan and, in his words, "Irish as Paddy's pig." Forty years later, they still hate each other.

Jack "Irish" Nicholson and Anjelica Huston. Once she tired of his drug-taking, philandering, sucking up to the Lakers, and lousy tipping habits, her own career took off.

THE IRISH: UNLUCKY IN LOVE
🐑 Part Two 🐑

The Irish are also capable of achieving romantic-domestic misery by seeking love *outside* the gene pool. These couples learned too late the perils of exogamy.

F. Scott Fitzgerald and Zelda Sayre. Although their relationship was legendarily horrible, she was his Southern belle, his preppie fantasy, and by marrying her Scott sought to distance himself from his shameful Mick origins. It was in his years at Princeton that he began, Gatsby-like, to deny his roots; as proof that he succeeded in doing so, in his will he requested "the cheapest possible funeral" for himself.

Joe Kennedy and Gloria Swanson. The smitten bootlegger turned movie producer liked to holiday with his mistress Gloria *and* his wife, Rose. Boston's Cardinal William O'Connell intervened; their film project *Queen Kelly* proved unreleasable, and Joe stuck Gloria with all the bills.

Lawrence of Arabia and Selim Amhed (aka Dahoum). Lawrence, whom his army mates dubbed "Short-arse," dedicated his *Seven Pillars of Wisdom* to this Arab boy. But since T.E. was repulsed by sex of any sort, one assumes their relationship was unconsummated.

Mary McCarthy and Edmund Wilson. The stunningly beautiful convent-educated author for totally mysterious reasons married and endured all sorts of abuse from the rotund grouch and literary critic known to all as "Bunny."

Scarlett O'Hara and Ashley Wilkes. The spunky Confederate colleen wasted her time pining away for a WASP wimp.

Ryan O'Neal and Farrah Fawcett. In an interview, the none-too-swift Ryan once expressed his doubts about his Irish ancestry: "I'm a Protestant," he explained. His relationship with the statuesque blonde featured plenty of fisticuffs.

Sean Penn and Madonna. One night when Sean had a snootful, he tied up his Italian-Catholic Material Girlfriend and fed her dog food. This episode is said to have inspired the nauseating "Erotica" video that Madonna later unleashed—so to speak—on the public.

Tyrone Power and Cesar Romero. Even dim-witted Lana Turner understood that Ty was bi when he gave her the brush-off to vacation with Romero in an airplane built for two; but prudish publicists suppressed news of the passion between the two studs of the silver screen.

Barbara Stanwyck and Robert Taylor. They set the standard for Hollywood "lavender" marriages, so it was a left hook to the kisser for the Irish Babs when Bob took up with an Italian (female) extra on the set of *Quo Vadis*.

Spencer Tracy and Katharine Hepburn. She—the proto-Yankee with an affected English accent—must have believed her liaison with the earthy Irish Tracy would give her that common touch. He may have proved *too* earthy the day she found him in his room in the Beverly Hills Hotel "unconscious, lying in his own filth"—a sight that doubtless prompted her to utter, "Oh, Spenc-aaah!"

Oscar Wilde and Lord Alfred Douglas. The Dublin genius was forced by his snotty British boytoy into a hopeless legal action, thereby ruining his life. In later years, Douglas, a married (!) man and convert to Catholicism (!!), called his former lover and benefactor "the lord of abominations" and "an old whore."

Abie's Irish Rose, a 1922 Broadway comedy, told the story of a Jewish-Irish romance. It ran for 2,327 performances, became a movie and radio serial, and inspired dozens of heartwarming movie and TV knockoffs. There have been more than a few real-life victims of the AIR syndrome:

Ruby Keeler and Al Jolson. Could a singing, dancing Irish girl from Hell's Kitchen possibly prove tough enough to survive marriage to an egomaniacal cantor's son in blackface? No.

Mia Farrow and Woody Allen. After seducing one of Mia's adopted daughters, Woody gushed in public about "what the heart wants." Through-out their child custody hearings, Maureen O'Sullivan's daughter fingered her rosary, dressed like a frump, and effectively set the image of Irish Catholic womanhood back to pre-famine days. Mia, who had turned on with the Beatles and married Frank Sinatra, had turned, before our very eyes, into Mother Machree!

Maron "Molly" and Leopold Bloom. Their marital sleeping arrangements were unorthodox, to say the least.

Neal Cassady and Allen Ginsberg. The poet fell hard for proto-Beat Cassady, ignoring the fact that the *On the Road* hero was a compulsive heterosexual. In the days before the term *sex addict* was the stuff of headlines, Cassady's daily sexual routine, peppered with a prodigious amount of self-abuse, included trysts with his wife, his girlfriend, and any chick he happened to meet. Ginsberg marveled at "the cocksman and Adonis from Denver," and in a moment of largesse, Cassady took him as a lover. After a few months, though, he hit the road, giving Ginsberg the go-by in a letter, apologizing, "I somehow dislike pricks and men." The poet was heartbroken but later claimed his despair inspired his writing and he dedicated his epic poem "Howl" to Cassady.

Gabriel Byrne and Ellen Barkin. Can an Irishman who studied for the priesthood find happiness with a Jewish girl from the Bronx who talks out of the side of her mouth? Apparently not.

SODOM AND BEGORRAH:
THE GAY IRISH

The scurrilous Greek historian Diodorus Siculus recorded than "among the Celts, the men are much keener on their own sex…they lie around on animal skins with a lover on each side." More recently, author Seán O'Faoláin defined "an Irish queer" as "a fellow who prefers women to drink."

For centuries, the Irish have had a low marriage rate, and among them, the lifelong conditions of bachelorhood and spinsterhood—not to mention clerical celibacy—are considered normal. Who are we to speculate as to the orientation of people who did nothing at all? Nevertheless, occasional cases have arisen.

In 1640, John Atherton, Anglican bishop of Waterford and Lismore, was hanged for the crime of sodomy.

Soldier, humanitarian, and patriot Roger Casement was one of the "martyrs" of the 1916 Easter Rising. Before hanging him, the Brits demolished his reputation by circulating his (possibly forged) diaries, in which he evidenced an unbecoming fascination with the organs of male Africans.

Married, Dublin-born dramatist Oscar Wilde served time in an English prison for his homosexuality; married, Dublin-born dramatist Brendan Behan claimed to have become homosexual in an English prison.

Dublin's popular Gate Theatre was founded seventy years ago by the gay couple of actor Micheal MacLiammóir and producer Hilton Edwards; at MacLiammóir's (televised) funeral in 1978, Irish president Patrick Hillery shook Edwards's hand and bravely uttered the traditional words of comfort to the widow, "I'm sorry for your trouble."

Homosexual acts were decriminalized in Ireland in 1993.

It has only recently been revealed that the late Tom Dooley, a missionary doctor to Laos once presented as a saintly role model to Irish-American parochial schoolchildren, took a distinctly unsaintly interest in little Laotian boys.

Uncloseted living Irish Americans include Patricia Ireland, the self-proclaimed bisexual head of NOW, and the feminist literary critic, lesbian, and occasional mental patient Kate Millett. Gay playwright Terrence McNally continues to act surprised at offending the people he sets out to offend.

The American Catholic Irish, of course, continue to be not only more Catholic than the pope but also more Jansenist than the Irish. In New York and Boston, Irish-American gays and lesbians are still forbidden to participate in St. Patrick's Day parades—in which, ironically enough, Irish-American sadists and pederasts are still permitted to march, under their traditional Christian Brothers banner...

CHAPTER 11

HOW TO BE WITTY AND CHARMING

They talked seriously of mocker's seriousness.

It has been observed that Jewish persons at present constitute a majority of American stand-up comics and comedy writers, and it has been suggested that their preeminence in the humor profession arises from their anomalous position in the nation's culture—they are immersed in it, but not yet altogether assimilated by it.

After 1800, the Irish stood in the same "in-but-not-of" relation to British culture, which may in part explain why Anglo-Irish writers produced so much classic "English" comedy of the eighteenth and nineteenth centuries: the plays of William Congreve, Richard Sheridan, Oscar Wilde, and George Bernard Shaw, and the prose satires of Richard Steele, Laurence Sterne, and Jonathan Swift.

Satire—hostile criticism, verbal abuse, insult —was an art form highly valued by the ancient Celts, whose kings employed poets, *bardai*, to taunt, ridicule, and, sometimes, to liquidate their enemies, by means of rhyming curses known as *ranns*. "I will not wish unto you...to be rhymed to death, as is said to be done in Ireland." (Sir Philip Sidney, *The Defence of Poesie*, circa 1582).

Swift, the dean of take-no-prisoners satire (as well as of Dublin's St. Patrick's cathedral), frequently cursed his enemies in rhyming *ranns*, and James Joyce's bitter 1912 poem "Gas from a Burner" is a more recent specimen:

> *...This lovely land that always sent*
> *Her writers and artists to banishment*
> *And in a spirit of Irish fun*
> *Betrayed her own leaders, one by one.*
> *'Twas Irish humour, wet and dry*
> *Flung quicklime into Parnell's eye...*

So, before setting yourself up as a witty Celt, be warned: in Irish tradition, a joke is a lethal (even suicidal) weapon.

When Parnell, in the midst of a messy divorce scandal, was attempting to assert control over the Irish members of parliament, he insisted, "I am still the master of this party." His fall from power was certain when, from the back of the room, his colleague Tim Healy hissed, "And who's the mistress?" Prosecuting Oscar Wilde for sodomy, Edward Carson asked him if he had ever kissed a boy named Walter Grainger. Oscar answered flippantly, "Oh, dear no. He was a peculiarly plain boy. He was, unfortunately, extremely ugly. I pitied him for it." And sealed his own fate.

SEA-DIVIDED GAELS OF LAUGHTER

In America, the newly arrived Irish realized they were being laughed at and, sensibly enough, began to charge admission. That is, they took to the stage—often in comedy teams. From 1850 through the turn of the century, headlining vaudeville performers included:

Neeham and Kelly ("The Roving Irish Gents")
Kelly and Ryan ("The Bards of Tara")
Rooney and Rogers ("The Galway Sluggers")
Collins and Hart ("The Bone Crunchers")
Mr. Duffy and Mr. Sweeney

⁓ and the famous ⁓

Mr. Gallagher and Mr. Shean of the 1922 Ziegfeld Follies

(Mr. Shean, it should be noted, was so un-Irish as to be the uncle of the Marx Brothers)

Micks took to the "legitimate" Broadway stage as well. **Eddie Foy** made his debut in *The Arabian Girl* in 1899, **George M. Cohan** with *The Governor's Son* in 1901 and **Pat Rooney, Sr.**, in *Nell to Go* in 1900, **Laurette Taylor** in *Peg o' My Heart* (1912), **Frank Fay** in *Girl o' Mine* (1918), and **Patsy Kelly** in *Delmar's Revels* (1927).

Among the early Irish-American authors of stage comedy were **Ned Harrigan**, who, between 1875 and 1893, wrote and costarred with **Tony Hart** in a series of hit "Mulligan Guard" knockabout revues at the Théâtre Comique; **George Kelly**, whose *Craig's Wife* won the 1926 Pulitzer, and **Marc Connelly**, whose *Green Pastures* won it in 1930. Even **Eugene O'Neill** wrote a comedy, *Ah Wilderness!*, in 1933. **Philip Barry**'s 1939 hit *The Philadelphia Story* returned to the stage, disguised as the musical *High Society*.

The fledgling recording industry was another medium for humor. **Russell Hunting**'s dialect "Casey" routines (including "Casey at the Bat") topped the charts five times between 1891 and 1894, and **Dan Kelly** (formerly of Christy's Minstrels) had three consecutive hit comic-monologue records in 1891.

Meanwhile, in films, slapstick comedy was being virtually *invented* by the Irish-American director **Hal Roach** and Irish-Canadian director **Mack Sennett** (né Michael Sinnott). Among the Irish silent-movie comic performers of genius were **Buster Keaton, Charlie Chaplin,** and **Mary Pickford.** Equally mute circus clown **Emmet Kelly** began performing as the hobo "Weary Willie" in 1923.

Arguably, radio's most brilliant comic writer-performer throughout the thirties and forties was ex-vaudevillian **John Florence Sullivan**, aka **Fred Allen**. Among his observations: *"Hollywood is a great place, if you're an orange,"* and *"The reason television is called a medium is because nothing on it is well done."*

Television *was* well done, nonetheless, by San Francisco–Irish comedienne **Gracie Allen**, as well as by a pair of Micks harking back to the fatty-n-skinny comedy teams of yore, **Jackie Gleason** and **Art Carney.**

But even in the New World, the "humor" of the Irish has inclined, as the late **Michael O'Donoghue** put it, "to draw blood." **Frank Fay** once refused Milton Berle's challenge to a "duel of wits" on the grounds that he would never fight an unarmed man. **J. P. Donleavy**'s hilarious and oft-censored novel *The Ginger Man* continues to offend generations of readers, while subversive comic **George Carlin** has been known to provoke howls of outrage with observations like *"I get the feeling Notre Dame came real close to naming itself 'The Fuckin' Drunken, Thick-skulled, Brawling, Short-dicked Irish."*

THE TRAGI-COMEDIAN

"There's nothing funnier than someone else's unhappiness," observes Nell, in Samuel Becket's *Endgame.*

Because he has been the victim of countless volumes of critical exegesis (mostly written by boiled owls), we sometimes forget that Beckett (like Joyce) was a *comic* author. His penchant for whimsical gallows humor extended to his personal life as well. Out for a walk with Sam on a glorious spring morning, a friend observed, *"It makes you glad to be alive!" "Oh,"* said Sam, *"I wouldn't go so far as that."* And when a French acquaintance enquired, *"Êtes-vous Anglais, Monsieur Beckett?"* he replied simply, *"Au contraire."*

PAT AND MIKE AND BRIDGET

All ethnic jokes are, of course, deplorable. But they have been around for a long time—the Greeks made them about the Boeotians. Sometimes, the butts of such jokes are stereotyped with a grudging admiration: the Jews (Izzy and Ikey) are invariably shrewd, and the Scot (Sandy) is practical, in a penny-pinching way.

WAY UP
MRS. GROGAN: "Mrs. Casey says her son Moike is way up in the polace departmint."
MRS. FLNN: "He is thot. His picther is on th' top row av th' rogues' gallery."

But the Irish Pat, Mike, and Bridget are simply fools, and "Irish" jokes are generally interchangeable with "polack" or "colored" ones.

On trial for theft, Pat and Mike rejoice to be found not guilty. Then Pat asks the judge, *"Does that mean we get to keep the money?"*

A crash is heard in the kitchen. *"Oh dear,"* **sighs the lady of the house.** *"More dishes, Bridget?"* **"No, ma'am,"** **comes the reply.** *"Fewer."*

CHAPTER 12

☙

HOW TO BE MISTY AND MYSTICAL

I was once the beautiful May Goulding. I am dead.

The Irish have a reputation for being un- or otherworldly, and those attempting to pass for Irish are advised to practice, in a mirror, affecting a dim, sad, faraway look in the eyes. In the case of an actual Irish person, this distracted, middle-distance stare usually signifies that he or she is carrying on a conversation with someone—a friend or relative—who happens no longer to be among the living.

It should be observed that **Halloween** was invented by the Celts. The Celtic New Year, *Samhain* (pronounced "Saw-een," for bonus points), falls on November first. On its eve, ancient pagan households and Druid priests would make human sacrifices to the lord of the dead, and on this night it was the custom of the deceased to leave their graves looking to inhabit a living body. Terrified Celts would light bonfires and dress up as demons and spooks to scare away these roving souls. On Samhain, the pooka haunted the crossroads and a nasty spirit named Muckolla would rear up to demand tribute and wreak havoc on the miserly. It was the famine immigrants who introduced Halloween to America, along with the Jack o' Lantern— although it was the Irish custom to insert a candle in a turnip, pumpkins being unavailable to them.

Ireland has long since dispensed with Samhain, human sacrifices, and even candles in turnips, but relationships between the living and the dead still remain oddly casual; the Catholic doctrine known as the Communion of Saints—which proposes a constant, lively interaction among earthbound mortals, the citizens of heaven, and the suffering souls in Purgatory—has appealed mightily to the Irish.

They are a race of people who want to go to heaven, whether they believe in it or not. At the same time, they fervently believe their dead, having departed this vale of tears, are never very far away. Even the ancient Gaels believed the souls lived in a parallel universe, the timeless Otherworld just below Ireland itself. Consider the story of a farmer who, refusing pots of money for a ruin near his house, explained, *"Ceard a dhean-fadh anamache me mhuinitire ansine?"* ("What would the souls of my ancestors do then?") A complex view of death, indeed, and nowhere more evident than in the social phenomenon known as the Irish Wake.

THE WAKE

The wake was created centuries ago for the benefit of the deceased, rather than, as it is today, a mourning process for the family. It provided breathing time, so to speak, between death and the moment the soul actually leaves the body—a period of time ranging from a few seconds to seventy-two hours. (Although it is reported that once, in Munster, a departed soul returned to have a brief chat with its former body during the wake.)

The first rule of wakes was never, ever to leave the body alone, and the second rule was to place it in familiar surroundings, preferably the kitchen. The corpse would be laid out on what was called a "hag bed" with a crucifix at the breast and a rosary in the hands.

It was expected that the entire village would arrive to drone decades of the rosary; laggards and no-shows would earn the lifetime enmity of the family. The bereaved would accommodate visitors with snuff, meat, whiskey, soda bread, clay pipes, and tobacco. The pipe would be passed, each inhaler ejaculating, *"The blessing of God on the souls of the dead."* Pipes and tobacco might later be thrown into the grave.

Traditional wakes combined reverence with merriment: storytelling, verse-making, tongue twisters, arm wrestling, and a rollicking game called "throw the potato." A foreign visitor once noted that Irish wakes could be "far more merrier than weddings." If cards were played, a hand would be placed in the fist of the deceased, and when the dancing began, it was not unusual to take the corpse for a quick spin around the kitchen.

Some sociologists, not familiar with the Irish psyche, have speculated that this behavior reflected a denial of death, a desperate attempt to stave off mortality. Wrong. It was actually a way of showing goodwill toward the deceased, whom, it was assumed, would stay involved in human affairs. A well-attended wake would placate any possible anger the corpse might have against the living.

The mourners would include professional "keeners," known as the Caoineadh, hired to perform their high-pitched wail and add a peculiar touch of showbiz to the wake. Their wail, not begun until after the soul had left the body, would weave a detailed narrative of the recently terminated life. As the bodies piled up during the famine years, keeners were unable to keep up with the demand, and went out of vogue—but not before inspiring this churlish bit of verse:

They live upon the dead,
By letting out their persons by the hour
To mimic sorrow when the heart's not sad

Wakes are still a major part of Irish cultural life, but the ritual differs depending on which side of the Atlantic you die on. In Ireland, the mortuary is generally right next to the church, and the chilly weather usually allows the family to forgo embalming. The natives, depending on their preference, drape their loved one in a shroud with a picture of the Sacred Heart or the Blessed Virgin Mary.

☕🐷 In America, among Irish of the Stage or Shanty classes, the stiff's garb is usually finery from a former Easter Sunday, and a unisex application of pancake makeup, rouge, and hairspray is apparent. American wakes are really *de facto* family reunions—mourners with coiffed hair come bearing pictures of recent weddings and with grandchildren in tow. Horseshoe-shaped floral arrangements are not uncommon, nor is the passing of business cards.

In both old and new countries, the traditional "I'm sorry for your trouble" greeting has been replaced by remarks that the deceased "looks like she's about to get up" or "Sure, he never harmed anyone." Anecdotes about the grand gal or fella buzz around the room. Alcohol, despite all the jokes by people who've never been to a wake, is never present. Grudges are still formed against no-shows, the parish priest still makes a brief appearance, and the rosary is said (either the Sorrowful or Glorious Mysteries).

🎩 Lace-Curtain wakes are of shorter duration, favor closed coffins, and offer nondenominational prayers instead of the rosary. In lieu of flowers, you are encouraged to make a contribution to the charity of your choice.

A SPOOK'S TOUR

Tash, theush, taibhse, sprid, and *scail* are a few Irish words for ghost. The nastier or livelier sort are poltergeists, most of whom died violent deaths. In recent Irish history, the most notable of these is the Coonian poltergeist, which tormented the Murphy family of County Fermanagh by snoring, farting, and pulling their bedclothes off. It was when the poltergeist started hissing the melodies of "The Soldier's Song" and "Boyne Water" that the disgusted Murphys finally emigrated to

America. Not surprisingly, given the importance of the tourist industry to the Irish economy, hauntings occur all around the country, and celebrity ghosts abound.

Killakee House, in the Wicklow Mountains, is the original site of the Hellfire Club, a gathering place for rascals of the Ascendancy class. Killakee has been haunted at various times by a crippled boy, two nuns, a dwarf, and a handsome Indian man. W. B. Yeats himself saw the ghost of the crippled boy, whom he believed to have been an unwilling participant in the blasphemous rituals of the club. As late as 1970, the current resident, Mrs. Margaret O'Brien, reported to the Dublin newspapers that ghosts had ransacked everything in the house except the holy water fonts.

Leap Castle in County Offaly is considered to be the most sinister building in Ireland. Apparitions there have included a shaven monk, a playboy, a lady in red, and a repulsive creature calling itself "It."

Clongowes Wood College (alma mater of James Joyce and known as the "Eton of Ireland") is haunted by a specter calling himself Marshall Browne. The ghost travels with a phantom dog.

St. Stephen's Green in Dublin is haunted by the ghost of one Buck Whaley, who was such a rascal that he played handball against the Wailing Wall in Jerusalem. Also haunted in Dublin are the **Olympia Theatre, Croke Park,** the **Shelbourne Hotel** (by a gabby girl ghost, Mary Masters), and the **Department of Foreign Affairs.**

Three students who occupied Room #3 of **Maynooth College**, the famous seminary, committed suicide. When an intrepid priest kept a vigil there, his healthy head of hair turned white overnight.

The ghost of a young girl seduced and killed by a squire haunts **Skryne Castle**, County Meath, in the foothills of Tara. She introduces herself as Mathilda.

The hills of western Tipperary are haunted by the ghost of a sheep and the farmer who loved him. They roam the fields by night, inseparable in death, *à la* Cathy and Heathcliffe.

T. E. Lawrence (Lawrence of Arabia) haunts **Killua Castle**, County Westmeath, the ancestral seat of his family, the Chapmans. Those who've seen him report that he's dressed all in white. El Aurens must be unhappy to be in the company of another Killua ghost, Jacky Dalton, a suicide famous in his lifetime for wearing an ill-fitting yellow wig.

W. B. Yeats mopes around **Renvyle House**, Galway, once a literary hotel run by his friend and physician Oliver St. John Gogarty. In his lifetime, Yeats held séances at Renvyle, and in recent years ghost hunter Sybil Leek has spotted the poet there. She reports that he's overdressed.

King James II is described by witnesses as a "disdainful-looking royal personage." He haunts the **River Boyne**, the site of his great defeat.

The ghost of Jonathan Swift stalks the halls of **St. Patrick's psychiatric hospital** in Dublin, a "mad house" he founded and endowed in his will, observing that no nation ever wanted it so much.

THE LITTLE PEOPLE

A subject to avoid in conversation with the natives is fairies. One of the most pervasive and offensive of Irish stereotypes is that they are universally superstitious. The odds that an ordinary Irish man or woman "believes" in the Good People, as they are commonly called, are no higher than that the average American "believes" that Elvis is still alive. About fifty-fifty, according to the latest polls.

Still, the Irish aren't taking any chances: When Shannon Airport was enlarging a runway, construction was rerouted, at great expense, rather than disturb a fairy settlement. In 1972, it made the news when Michael O'Shea found and produced some fairy clothing, a tiny waistcoat with silver buttons and a pair of breeches of similar size.

The **fairies** of Ireland are angels who fell from heaven during Lucifer's long-ago war with God, and were lucky enough to land in Ireland. Do not refer to all Irish fairies as *leprechauns*. As a class, the latter are quite rare—being individuals employed as shoemakers by the many indigenous Hibernian supernatural beings known collectively as the *sidh* (pronounced "shee").

The **sidh** were descended from the goddess Danu and therefore are sometimes called the **Tuatha de Danaan** (Danaan's people). Diminished by Christianity to the status of fairies, they inhabit mounds and *raths* (forts); they have bodies that are like clouds.

Leprechauns—also known as lubricans—are to be distinguished from **cluricaunes**, who are fairy brewers and drunkards, and the **Fir Darrig**, who are given to japes and jests. All these creatures are solitaries, or loners, and dress in red—unlike the more common "trooping" fairies, the **siofra** (say "sheaf-ra"), who wear green and travel in gangs. It is they who steal children and cast spells (*pishogues*).

The wails of the **banshee** (*bean sidh*) foretell death and are heard only by those of pure Celtic blood. Banshees resemble disheveled women with long, unkempt hair and bony fingers. Certain family lines have their own personal banshee.

The **pooka, phouka,** or **puka** is a malevolent spirit who lurks in rocks, takes the shape of a black dog, horse, goat, or bull, and has been known to carry its victims off on a madcap ride. The most famous pooka of modern times, a fiendish black shape-shifting hound, frequents an area called Pussy Leap, outside Dublin. A ghost horse with a homely human face, hailing from County Louth, made the news in 1966 after terrifying several law-abiding and allegedly sober citizens.

The **roane** are half-seal, half-human. **Merrows** are beautiful mermaids, despite having fishtails and scaly fingers, or repulsive mermen with green teeth, green hair, pig's eyes, and red noses.

The **grogan** is a squat, hairy preternatural creature native to Ulster.

The **gruagach** are hairy ogres who will, if bribed, look after cattle.

We repeat: avoid mention of these creatures when in conversation with the locals, lest you give offense, or, still worse, have your ear talked off.

THE CELTIC TWILIGHT AND THE GOLDEN DAWN

New Age culture has appropriated Celtic traditions with an enthusiasm not seen since this same group hijacked the ancient customs of unsuspecting Native Americans. It was inevitable that Celtic culture, abundant as it is with goddesses, circles (Celts, being notoriously nonlinear, love circles), wisewomen, nature poetry, sacred places, and chanting, would appeal to the esoterics of the New Age. "Druid" rituals, stories of Tir-nan-Og, the Land of Eternal Youth, and the sexy, violent myths of the Tuatha de Danaan all are easily adapted to late twentieth-century ersatz mysticism's cult of narcissistic blather, with what can only be termed harmonic convergence:

⊙ **Crystals.** They were originally called Druid stones and used as transmitters to send messages to the Otherworld.

Druids. The role the Druids played in pre-Christian Ireland suggests that the Irish were a priest-ridden race long before Christianity came along. However, Druid priests—unlike their Christian successors—included both intellectuals and women in their ranks.

Irish Christianity was able to flourish because it adapted Celtic beliefs, rather than trying to obliterate them. Christian missionaries baptized, as it were, the holy mountains, sacred oaks, and holy wells (vestigial shrines to forgotten water spirits), making them their own, and more than a few Celtic gods and goddesses embarked on second careers as saints of the church.

The Goddess. The role of a Divine Female is nothing less than an obsession with New Agers, and so it was for the ancient Celts as well. The Druid Amairgen promised the goddess Eire that children of the Gael would use her name as the principal name of their country, and in return Ireland would always be "in the body" of this goddess. Today, tourists in Eire with a penchant for New Age culture should check out the Temple of Isis in Wexford.

Healers and Homeopathy. Ireland has a long tradition of healers, such as the superhero Finn MacCool, who could cure people by bringing them water held in his hands. In the nineteenth century Biddy Early, a famous healer and clairvoyant, employed herbs and mystical powers. (Biddy was also renowned for medical consultations with fairies and her many, younger husbands.) Today, homeopathic healers, of both cattle and people, flourish in all parts of Ireland. The most famous healer today, attracting thousands to her Achill Island home, is Marie Gallagher, an ex-nun. "Wellness" vacations are taken in Laughaurone and Kilcullen. The sacred wells of the Celts became the holy wells of the Christians, but today people still visit them for their former, pagan powers. A pilgrim selects a well based on its specialty, and seeks relief by walking around it several times, preferably counterclockwise.

👹 **May Day.** Anyone who has witnessed a New Age May Day festival with its celebrants bouncing around a maypole and braying chants should be reminded that this was a tradition born of pagan—Druid—Ireland. May first was called Beltaine, and the ancient Irish celebrated it with bon fires, dancing, and nooky. (Christian Ireland changed it into a celebration of the Blessed Virgin Mary.)

👹 **New Age Music.** A cursory glance at the New Age section in record stores reveals a preponderance of Irish artists and/or themes: John Doan (*Eire*), David Arkenstone (*A Celtic Book of Days*), Patrick O'Hearn, Loreena McKennit, Leahy, Altan, Clannad, De Danaan, Anam, Anuna, Eden, Christy O'Leary, and the high priestess of New Age wailing: Enya.

👹 **Shamanism.** The epic confrontation at Tara between St. Patrick and a Druid priest was a battle of opposing fire ceremonies—Easter against Beltaine. They were, in effect, dueling shamans. And shamanism is, of course, a cornerstone of New Age religions and pretensions.

👹 **The Soul.** Of the numerous best-selling self-help books about the soul (an entity on which ancient and modern Celts share a common fixation) one of the most popular is *Anam Cara* (Gaelic for "soul friend"), by Father John O'Donahue. It addresses the Celtic passion for the divine and reverence for the soul, which encompasses the body, not vice versa. *Anam Cara* promises that "The ancient wisdom, poetry and blessings of Celtic spirituality will awaken and grace the beauty of your heart's landscape."

👹 **Trees.** The ancient Celts were the original tree huggers. The oak was part of sacred rituals and they thought "everything that grows on oaks has been sent from heaven by the gods." The rowan is considered lucky. The hawthorn, another sacred bush, was believed to be the home of the fairies, and even today the government is careful not to disturb hawthorn bushes when mapping out new roads.

It should be pointed out

that W. B. Yeats was not only the finest English-language poet of the century, but also the first New Ager. Nothing magical, mystical, or occult was too goofy for him to try: Ouija boards, automatic writing, hashish sessions, encounters with ghosts, seers, fairies, gurus, neoplatonism… His excursions into Theosophy, and his later initiation into a magical fraternity based on Rosicrucianism and known as the Golden Dawn, reflected the archpoet's obsession with all things spiritual—except, of course, Christianity, which was so…*vulgar.*

The torch, as it were, has been passed to today's Aidan Kelly, who is the founder of what is called the New, Reformed, Orthodox Order of the Golden Dawn.

CHAPTER 13

IF YOU EVER GO
ACROSS THE SEA TO IRELAND

There were equally excellent opportunities for
vacationists in the home islands, delightful sylvan spots
for rejuvenation, offering a plethora of attractions.

GEOGRAPHY

Take a look at that colorful souvenir tea towel—the one
with the bogus map of the "Irish clans" on it. You'll notice,
maybe, that the entire island is divided into four provinces (aka
"Four Green Fields") and further subdivided into thirty-two
counties. The large southern area—doubt-
less colored green—is variously known as
"the republic" (which is a euphemism) and
Eire (which is unpronounceable). The
smaller northern section—usually tinted
pink—will be labeled either "Northern Ireland" or, erroneously, "Ulster."

(Three counties of the historic king-
dom of Ulster—Cavan, Donegal and Monaghan—in fact belong to the republic).

You will search the map in vain for Finian's euphonious
Clockamorra, but there are plenty of real place-names with sim-
ilar lyric charm. Then there are others, areas perhaps of great
beauty, but with hideous names: Ardfert (Kerry), Ballybunnion
(Kerry), Ben Bulbin (Sligo), Benwee Head (Mayo), Bloody
Foreland (Donegal), Bunratty Castle, the Dingle, Feacle
(Clare), Gorey (Wexford), Knockninny (Fermanagh), the Loo
valley, Offaly, the Ow River (Wicklow), Portlick Castle (West-
meath), Puffing Hole (Clare), and the River Suck (Galway).
Black Head pops up in both Antrim and Clare.

If you are determined to pass for Irish, you must visit Ireland at least once, in order to refer to "the last time I was over."

And it's the least you can do—tourist dollars constitute 7 percent of the Irish GNP; the industry gives full-time employment to 100,000 natives, who would otherwise be tempted to come over here looking for work.

🐷 It may be assumed that tourists of the Shanty Irish class will stay with relatives, bringing about a happy conjunction of traditional American schnorring with traditional Irish hospitality.

"IRELANDLAND"

🎩☕ Goodly news, goodly news! (Stage and Lace-Curtain Irish only need apply). It is now possible to tour Erin's Green Isle without encountering or experiencing the actual place at all! A sort of theme park, hereinafter known as **Irelandland**, consists of *Killarney, Tralee, the Ring of Kerry,* and other areas featuring *"jaunting"* cars; *Bunratty Castle* and all places likewise advertised as *"medieval"*; the *Blarney Stone*; *Jury's Cabaret*; the *"Quiet-Man Tour"*; a visit to *Kate Kearney's Cottage*; a tour-guided *"Dublin Pub Crawl"*; and plenty o' time for shopping at the *Shannon Airport* souvenir shop.

Accommodations in Irelandland include air-conditioned, cable-ready prestressed concrete rental units appearing to be of clay and wattles made, complete with faux-thatched roofs; or, for the truly rich, reconditioned castles (e.g., Ashford, Adare, and Drumoland) filled with other tourists who look like friends of the Reagans.

GOLF IRELAND:
ON THE GREEN IN THE GREEN

So many Americans go over to Ireland for the golf that the Irish Tourist Board has taken to running glossy magazine ads that show nothing but golf courses. Travel agents now promote Ireland as the alternative to the golfers' Mecca, Scotland itself. Tiger Woods recently made a triumphant tour.

But be advised: In Ireland, it's not just the Ascendancy blokes who play. The Irish of all classes are enthusiastic hackers. The natives tend to wear more informal and subdued outfits than do the visitors, eschew caddies and carts, and take swings with fags hanging out of their mouths.

There are more than three hundred golf courses and hundreds of driving ranges scattered throughout Ireland, some of them featuring such curious hazards as the ruins of ancient monasteries and casual grazing cattle. The elite are: Royal Portrush in Antrim; Ballybunnion Golf Club in Kerry (the favorite course of Bill Clinton); Waterville House, likewise in Kerry (which was the site of secret masses in penal times); Mount Juliet in Kilkenny; Royal County Down; Portmarnock (Dublin); The K Club (Kildare); County Louth Golf Club; County Sligo Golf Club; and Lahinch (Clare).

TIPS FOR THE TOURIST

■ Any brochure will advise you that the Irish drive on the left-hand side of the road. This is not true. The Irish drive in the middle of the road, and—without warning—stop there, too.

■ Do not—however lost you are bound to become—ask directions of a native. Although they mean well, they never point (it's rude) but rather use head nods as indicators. Then there's the difficulty in distinguishing left from right. So the best you can hope for is a vague "over there," if not a considered, reluctant "I'd start from somewhere else."

■ If you see a pile of litter by the side of the road, roll up the windows. You are approaching a "halting site," that is, an enclave of Travellers, a wandering tribe of folk formerly known as Tinkers.

■ When the temperature goes above 50, it is deemed by the natives to be "close." Over 60, it's called "roasting." When it's raining, it's "soft."

■ Be prepared to have total strangers act not simply as if you are lifelong friends, but as if you were both picking up a conversation interrupted the day before yesterday.

■ Do not, outside the narrow boundaries of rarefied Dublin 4, expect to find any of the following: bikini wax, dental implants, wellness issues, decaf latte, sun-dried tomatoes, *Playboy* magazine, nose jobs, or nose-hair clippers. (Nose rings, however, are popular in Galway.)

■ At all times, know and respect the local culture and belief systems. For instance: There is a terrifying, surreal colored picture—which appears to represent a doleful hippie ripping his chest open—tacked to every wall. It represents the "Sacred Heart of Jesus." Pass no remarks. Frequently it is accompanied by the black-and-white image of a hairy-nosed gaffer, his hands wrapped in bloody bandages. He is Padre Pio (né Francesco Forgione, 1887–1968). Do not ejaculate, "Holy cow, what happened to him?" He was blessed with the stigmata and could work miracles; for example, appearing in two places at once. (Curiously, he never employed this gift to visit his many devoted Irish fans.) Richard Gere is also popular.

■ In restaurants unless you're in Ballymalloe House or some other showplace of the "New Irish Cuisine"—do not ask your waitperson, "How's that cooked?" The question is considered queer, nosy, and downright rude.

■ While in conversation with a native, remember to observe the age-old Celtic taboo against self-promotion. (Don't be confused by the example of self-proclaimed "Lord of the Dance" Michael Flatley. He was born in Chicago.) Do not, therefore, brag. Especially, don't brag about your children. It's bad luck.

■ Avoid, if possible, the malodorous city of Limerick, the stinky county of Leitrim and the town of Ballinasloe in Galway, which reeks of rendered fat.

■ Don't try to bargain—it's considered barbaric. The Irish are embarrassed enough about money to begin with.

■ Keep your musical opinions to yourself. Garth Brooks is a minor deity in Ireland, as was John Denver before him. Centuries ago, Irish immigrants brought with them their ballads and reels to the American South. Now, Celtic music has returned to Ireland, bastardized and plasticized, and it is way more popular there than Irish "traditional" music.

■ Never say any of the following: **Begorrah! Faith and...; Top o' the morning; Saints preserve us! Up the Rebels! or Erin go bragh!** You will be exposed as a Yank and a cornball.

■ President Bill Clinton is adored and all his sins of the flesh have been forgiven by the Irish people: "Sure he didn't know what he was doing."

When in the South

💼 Don't be talking about the "Troubles." The citizens of the republic act as if all incidents in the North were transpiring in Zimbabwe. When in the North, please refer to the following:

Up in Ulster

💼 Don't use the term "The Troubles." Catholics call it "the war" or "the struggle," and Protestants don't want to talk about it at all. The Catholics and Protestants look alike—which is to say, they all look Irish—but there are ways to tell them apart. For example, Protestants are better dressed, and are likely to refer to England as "the Mainland." Catholics in the North are, if possible, more reserved than their coreligionists in Eire. All taxi drivers are Protestants and all black persons are British soldiers.

Protestants	Catholics
Say "Londonderry"	Say "Derry"
Say "the Province"	Say "the Six Counties"
Call the IRA "Provos" or "terrorists"	Call the IRA "the lads"
Call the Department of Health and Social Services "the DHSS"	Call the Department of Health and Social Services "the D *Haitsh* SS"
Are named Alan, Gordon, Kenneth, Doreen, Elaine, Ruth	Are named Seamus, Joseph, Patrick, Bernadette, Bridget, Mary

Regardless of denomination, God is big in Northern Ireland. In a population of 1.5 million, only 64 people call themselves atheists.

N.B.: Even if you're a Farsi Indian, stay out of Northern Ireland on July 12. And the day before. And the day after.

CHAPTER 14

✿

ROLE MODELS

*What two temperaments
did they individually represent?
The scientific. The artistic.*

It may console you to know that in order to be Irish, you need not pose as a Big Thinker. Neither at home nor in the diaspora do the Irish have reputations as intellectuals—that is, scientists or philosophers. Nor is this surprising. For a century, 1695 until 1793, the Penal Laws imposed by the English denied a majority of the native Irish the right to any education at all; thereafter, their schooling was undertaken by Christian Brothers and Ursuline Sisters, whose institutions were hardly hotbeds of intellectual stimulation.

Likewise, in the New World, the "separate" or "parochial" schools which Irish immigrants insisted upon their right to attend did not have the production of free-thinking astrophysicists as a pedagogical objective.

Yet the Irish persist, with some justification, in referring to their homeland as an "Isle of Saints and Scholars," for they know that their ancestors "saved civilization"—or had "been illuminating manuscripts while the English were still hanging from trees by their tails," as the saying went. And now, thanks to the published work of Thomas Cahill (God love him), the holy missionary scholars of ancient Hibernia are getting their worldwide due.

Likewise, the proverbial saintliness of the Irish was ignored by the Vatican for 750 years. Although millions of persecuted men and women steadfastly and heroically clung to their faith through several centuries, not a single Irish man or woman was officially declared to be a saint from the 1225 canonization of St. Lawrence O'Toole until that of St. Oliver Plunket in 1975.

SAINTS AND SCHOLARS

Saint Attracta (fifth century) A beautiful pagan-princess-turned-nun, Attracta was consecrated by St. Patrick himself, who was handed her veil directly from heaven. Attracta once vanquished a monster by stuffing a cross into its jaws; her chariot was drawn by a team of tame deer. Feast Day, August 11.

George Berkeley (1685–1753) The world-famous double-domed Empiricist philosopher (in whose honor the California university is named) was a Church of Ireland prelate, born in Kilkenny.

Saint Boclan (circa fifth century) As an infant, he was prematurely buried by his mother, who fortunately had the sense to dig him up when he cried out from the grave. As a grown-up bishop, he ran afoul of St. Patrick for his indiscriminate baptism of Irish pagans, but they patched it up. Feast Day, February 20.

Robert Boyle (1627–91) The noted chemist (who formulated Boyle's Law) was born in Waterford at Lismore Castle.

Saint Brigid (fifth century) A transcendent figure of Christian and even pre-Christian Ireland, Brigid possessed the "fanatic heart" of Irish lore. The daughter of a chieftain (or some dare say, a Druid priest), Brigid was exceedingly beautiful. In a desperate attempt to rid herself of troublesome admirers, Brigid prayed for deformity and had an instant attack of a fifth-century version of the Elephant Man disease. Her father took one look at Brigid and hastily agreed to her becoming a nun. Angels shoved the priest aside to personally present her with her nun's veil and, at the same time, restore her beauty. Brigid became a bishop and founded several convents, churches, and (coed!) monasteries. In her spare time, she would make beer from her bathwater, dance with foxes, and reconcile armies at war. Though she gave her Christian name to centuries of Irish girls, St. Brigid is now known as the "Mary and Juno of the Gael." Feast Day, February 1.

Saint Columbanus (543–615) A light unto the Dark Ages, this brawny but learned monk traveled across barbaric Europe establishing monasteries and schools, thereby preserving and/or reestablishing Civilization as We Know It. Feast Day, November 23.

Saint Columba, or **Columcille** (521–597) A poet-booklover-warrior-monk, he stole off at night to make a copy of a psalter (aided by the five fingers of his left hand, which shone while he copied). King Diarmaid found out and, in history's first copyright case, ordered Columba to return the book, causing him no end of humiliation. The saint found a specious excuse to mobilize his brawny kinsmen against the king and defeated Diarmaid in a great victory that was most unbecoming for a man of God. The contested psalter was preserved by Columba's tribe and renamed, not surprisingly, *Cathach* or "Warrior." It is the oldest surviving manuscript in Western Europe. Feast Day, June 9.

Edward Dowden (1843–1913) This Trinity College don's 1875 volume *Shakespeare: A Critical Study of His Mind and Art* has influenced all subsequent biographies of the Bard.

Saints Ethenia the Fair and **Fidelmia the Rosy** Daughters of the high king, they encountered St. Patrick soon after his arrival in Ireland, and were baptized by him. Moreover, they were consecrated nuns that very same day, promptly died, and went immediately to heaven. Feast Day, January 11.

William Rowan Hamilton (1805–65) This Dublin-born mathematician introduced into algebra the theory of quaternions, and discovered both the phenomenon of conical refraction and the "Hamilton function," upon which Einstein is said to have based his famous Theory of Relativity.

Saint Ita The "Brigid of Munster" was an abbess who kept a school for boys and became known as the "foster mother of saints." One of her charges was St. Brendan, who consulted her before making his famous voyage to discover America. When a young nun in her charge became pregnant, the compassionate Ita claimed and reared the child as her own. Feast Day, January 15.

Theresa Kearney, Mother Kevin (1875–1957) A missionary to Uganda, she established schools, hospitals, orphanages, and even —her masterstroke—a village for lepers. Although she was buried in Ireland, the Ugandans begged the Irish government for the return of her body—and then gave Mother Kevin the biggest funeral in East African history. Her name has passed into the Ugandan language, where *kevin* means a hospital, or any work of mercy.

Maura "Soshin" O'Halloran (1955–83) After studying at Trinity College, Dublin, she traveled to Tokyo, there to train for the monastic life—as a Buddhist nun. At the Toshoji, where she was the only foreigner and only female in residence, she was given the name Soshin (warm heart). She wrote in her journal, "I am named Soshin. I like it. It rhymes with Oisin." After becoming a Zen master, she was on her way back to Ireland when she was killed in an accident in Thailand. Her statue was erected in the Kannonji monastery, as a sign that she had achieved sainthood, and was "of the same heart and mind as the Great Teacher Buddha."

Saint Patrick The fifth-century British-born missionary bishop who first successfully introduced Christianity to Ireland was a saint, but no scholar. To judge from his extant writings, such as his *Confession,* his Latin was bad, and his Gaelic was worse. Patrick will have the privilege of judging, the entire Irish race at the end of time. Feast Day, March 17.

John Scotus "Erigena" (810–77) Irish-born, as his name indicates, this theologian, philosopher, wit, and linguist held the position of head of the Palace School in the Frankish court of Charles II.

Saint Senan A sixth-century bishop and former pagan warrior, he drove a dragon from Scattery Island in the River Shannon. Pebbles gathered from the site are believed to be efficacious against shipwreck. Feast Day, March 8.

Enid Starkie (1897–1970) Born in Killiney, County Dublin, she became an honorary Fellow of Oxford, as an authority on French literature. She wrote definitive biographies of Rimbaud and Baudelaire.

William Thomson, Lord Kelvin (1874–1907) This engineer, mathematician, and physicist, whose contributions to science include the temperature scale named after him, was born in Belfast.

Ernest Walton (1903–95) The codeveloper of the first successful nuclear particle accelerator and cowinner of the 1951 Nobel Prize for physics was a native of Waterford and professor at Trinity College in Dublin.

BIDDIES, BROADS, AND BALLBUSTERS

Doff that shawl, drop that rosary, and for the love of Mike stop that infernal keening! To Irish and would-be Irish women we recommend the following alternatives to the tired old Mother Machree act.

Nora Barnacle (1884–1951) Preferring lighter fare, the wife of James Joyce declined to read his work—yet their grandson is certain that the master "could have done none of it, written not one of his books without her." The events of Joyce's novel *Ulysses* take place on the day—June 16, 1904—when he and Nora first met, and she treated the virginal bard to a hand job.

Laura Bell (mid-19th century) From humble beginnings as a Belfast shop girl, she went on to become one of the most successful prostitutes in London. In 1850, Prince Jung Bahadur of Nepal gladly paid £250,000 for a single night in her company.

Alice Crimmins (1940–) Once, the mention of her name sent a chill through the heart of every parochial-school-teaching nun. The image of American Irish-Catholic womanhood has never recovered from the shock. Alice must have been absent from her Bronx school the day the nuns read from the Baltimore Catechism about the mortally sinful tongue kiss and the runaway train, for she seems to have graduated with her libido intact. The lurid details of her love life—her paramours included various Italians, her boss at a cocktail lounge, and her children's barber, for the love of God!—came out in her trial for the murder of her two young children. The evidence was inconclusive, but Alice was found guilty—perhaps because she appeared in court in a bouffant hairdo with little bows on the side, a miniskirt, and white stockings. For an Irish girl, white stockings are seldom a wise fashion choice.

☠ **Bernadette McAliskey (née Devlin)** (1947–) When still a college student in Belfast, she became a pivotal figure in the Northern Irish civil rights struggle, earning from her enemies the titles of "Pope's Whore" and "Fidel Castro in a miniskirt." At twenty-one, she was elected to the British Parliament, where, in the aftermath of "Bloody Sunday," she physically assaulted Tory minister Reg Maudling. In 1981, she, her children, and her husband, Michael McAliskey, were shot by Protestant paramilitaries in their home. "We've been fighting eight hundred years just to bring a system of justice to this country and for eight hundred years they've jailed us…I've brought a child of my own into the world, and I'm convinced she'll live to see the society we're trying to build." Her daughter, Roisin, gave birth in an English prison.

☠ **Devorgilla (Dearbhforgaill)** (1108–93) While her devout husband was away on a pilgrimage, Queen Devorgilla (then in her late forties) chanced to meet with the (sixty-four-year-old) Dermot MacMurrough. Their attraction was mutual, but the chivalrous Dermot went through the motions of "abducting" her; when the outraged husband returned, he went after the pair with an army. Dermot appealed to the (English) Normans for aid. The Normans came—and never left. Devorgilla is said to have taken refuge in the Abbey of Mellifont, County Louth, and died "lamenting that she had brought so many evils on her country."

☠ **Elizabeth Gurley Flynn** (1890–1964) Joe Hill wrote his song "The Rebel Girl" in her honor. She joined the Industrial Workers of the World in 1906, and helped organize strikes in Lawrence, Massachusetts, in 1912 and Paterson, New Jersey, in 1913. After being repeatedly arrested and jailed for her speeches, she cofounded the American Civil Liberties Union in 1920—from which organization she was duly expelled in 1940, after she became a member of the Communist Party. A columnist for *The Daily Worker*, she was imprisoned, from 1955 to 1957, for her "seditious" politics, and upon her release elected chairman of the Party. The Rebel Girl died on a visit to Moscow, and was treated to a spectacular funeral in Red Square.

☠ **Rose O'Neal Greenhow** (1814–64) A heroine of the Confederacy, her rabid racism may have resulted from her father's murder at the hands of a slave. Before the war, Rose held court at her Washington boardinghouse, flirting with congressmen. She may have taken things further with John C. Calhoun, about whom she gushed, "He's the wisest man of the century."

Once hostilities commenced, she became a Confederate spy, flashing secret hand signals from her bedroom window and strutting around Washington with battle plans concealed in her hairdo. Rose sailed to Europe to raise funds for the cause, and upon her return ran into the Union blockade. Undaunted, she hopped into a rowboat and might have escaped—but the gold coins she had sewn into her dress caused the boat to sink, and Rose to drown.

Mary "Mother" Jones (1830–1930)

Known as "America's Joan of Arc" and "the Miners' Angel," she was born Mary Harris, in Cork, and emigrated to the United States in the famine years. In 1867, in Tennessee, she lost her husband and four children to yellow fever. In '71, when her home and business were destroyed in the Chicago fire, she turned for help to the Knights of Labor, and soon began to take an active, and highly visible, part in the labor movement, traveling the nation on behalf of the United Mine Workers, organizing, supporting strikes, and agitating against "the crime of child labor." Her slogans were "Join the Union, boys!" and "Pray for the dead but fight like hell for the living!"

Alice Kyteler (fl. 1324)

Traditionally, Irish society has given its witches the respect they deserve, but in the case of Alice—a Kilkenny matron of Flemish descent who had buried four husbands—an English-born (wouldn't you know it?) bishop insisted on an arrest and trial. The chief witness for the prosecution was Petronilla, a serving maid. She swore she had seen Ms. Kyteler enjoying the company of her lover, "Robin Mac Art," a demon who was wont to materialize in the form of "three Negroes." Alice wisely fled to England, and the frustrated bishop had to be satisfied with executing Petronilla.

Lady Hazel Lavery (1880–1935)

Hazel was an American beauty married to the Anglo-Irish painter Sir John Lavery. Her portrait—as a somewhat startled-looking Cathleen Ni Houlihan—adorned the Irish pound note from 1928 to 1975. During the negotiations that ended the Irish rebellion, she was instrumental in bringing Winston Churchill and Michael Collins together for dinner, the latter staying for breakfast. At the funeral for the assassinated Collins, Hazel appeared in widow's weeds and dissolved into hysterics, throwing her rosary into the grave. This raised some eyebrows, since she was married to someone else, he was engaged to someone else, the rosary was made of real pearls...and she wasn't even a Catholic.

♣ **Eliza Lynch** (1830–86) Fleeing the potato famine, she descended on Paraguay and proved to be a blight on that nation's history once she became the mistress to the dwarf-dictator Francisco Solano López. "The Paraguayan Pompadour," as she was known, inspired him with dreams of empire, and the resulting five-year-long war reduced his country's male population by 90 percent. It was said that a statue of the Virgin wept whenever Eliza entered the cathedral of Asunción. Perhaps the BVM had got wind of the fact that she had already pocketed gems belonging to the Virgin of Caapacu. Eliza was eventually portrayed, on Argentinian radio, by Eva "Evita" Perón.

☠ **Finola MacDonnell (aka Inion Dubh)** (sixteenth century) Daughter of a powerful Scottish highland clan, she married Hugh, lord of Tirconnell, kept him in power through the use of her Scottish mercenaries ("redshanks"), then had him deposed in favor of her son "Red Hugh." After the English victory at Kinsale (1601) and the "Flight of the Earls," Finola shrewdly turned in Hugh's nemesis, Niall Garbh O'Donnell, to the conquerors. He got life in the Tower of London, she got six hundred acres in the Ulster plantation.

☠ **Maeve (or Medhbh)** (first century A.D.) She persuaded her father to set her up as queen of Connaught, with the intention of establishing a matriarchy. As a married woman, she tried to persuade her husband, Ailill, that she was grander than he (she was) and their spat resulted in the epic struggle described in the Tain Bo Culaigne. In her determination to acquire a bigger bull than Ailill's, she was not shy about offering her "friendly thighs" to the likes of the prodigiously virile hero Fergus. Maeve (whose name means "intoxicating") had many lovers, and boasted that she was "never without one man in the shadow of another." She required that her mates be "without niggardliness, without jealousy, and without fear," and refused to let any king rule Tara who had not first mated with her. She lived to 120, only to be felled by a piece of hard cheese while bathing.

♣ **"Typhoid Mary" Mallon** (1855–1938) This recent Irish immigrant to America realized it wasn't sheer coincidence that typhoid fever broke out in any household where she was employed as a cook—so she hustled from city to city, changing her identity. By the end of her run, she was responsible for twelve epidemics, one of which killed 1,400 people. Tracked down by health inspectors, she refused to surrender, attacking the do-gooders with a meat cleaver. Once captured, she was declared a medical marvel. Her stool was teeming with lethal typhoid salmonella, but Mary had never missed a day's work. Today, her legacy lives on, wherever a sign is posted urging employees to "wash hands before leaving bathroom."

☠ Countess Constance Markievicz (née Gore-Booth) (1868–1927)

Yeats described her and her sister Eva Gore-Booth as "both beautiful, one a gazelle." Eva was the gazelle. "Con," who all her life pronounced her homeland "Ahland," was a socialite and dilettante, married to a Polish count. Suddenly, at forty, she threw herself into the Republican cause. (When she was made an officer in the Citizen Army, O'Casey resigned from it.) In the Easter Rebellion, she manned—so to speak—a machine-gun in St. Stephens Green. After her death sentence was commuted, the countess served as minister of labor in the first Dail, and was the first woman elected to the British House of Commons—in which she refused to serve. Although she died in poverty, she was afforded the showiest Irish funeral ever given a woman, her coffin followed through the streets of Dublin by eight truckloads of flowers.

☠ Lola Montez (Marie Dolores Gilbert) (1818–61)

Her lovers were legion, her husband was gouty, but it was during her stint as mistress of King Ludwig I of Bavaria that Lola achieved international recognition. The king announced that in one twenty-four-hour period the agreeable flamenco-dancing colleen from Limerick had visited ten orgasms upon him. He marveled that she could "perform miracles with the muscles of her private parts." Lola was easy, but not without her standards. She gave the brushoff to the Polish viceroy, who suffered from denture breath. She spent her twilight years in America, counseling "fallen women" and no doubt sharing with them a tale or two.

☠ Mary O'Brien (Maire Rue O'Brien) (1615–86)

When Connor, her husband and the father of her eight children, was killed by the invading British army, the pragmatic Mary, in order to save her life, wooed and married one of Cromwell's officers. She soon did away with this distasteful Puritan husband, but raised one of her sons as a Protestant in order to keep the family estate in the family. Today her castle, Drumoland, serves as luxury lodgings for rich American tourists.

❧ **Sinéad O'Connor** (1966–) As pop singer with a concentration-camp hairstyle, she first made headlines in 1992, when she vigorously encouraged Albert Renyolds, the Irish prime minister, to get involved in the case of "Miss X," a fourteen-year-old rape victim then attempting to obtain an abortion. Thirty million American TV viewers (who failed to take offense at Madonna on all fours being led around on a leash) were horrified when Sinéad tore up a picture of the pope and called the Catholic Church "an evil empire built on lies."

❧ **Grace O'Malley (alias Granuaile)** (1530–1630) The daughter of a chieftain in the west, she married a like spirit, the pirate Dan O'Flaherty. Together they plundered British merchant ships off the stormy Connemara coast. Sword in hand, Grace always took part in the fighting—even the day after giving birth. When her beloved husband was killed, she remarried and persuaded her new (and equally beloved) mate Richard ("Iron Dick") Bourke to join her in her profession of pirating. Together, they acquired so vast an estate for the O'Malleys that when Grace met Elizabeth I (in 1593) they spoke as equals, queen to queen. The most amazing aspect of her life is that it was never made into a 20th Century Fox swashbuckler, starring Susan Hayward.

❧ **Louisa O'Murphy, "La Morphil"** (circa 1740–?) A plump young beauty—the Goncourts described her as "a merry Rubens"—she was an apprentice seamstress who modeled on the side for artist François Boucher. King Louis XV first laid eyes on her in Boucher's painting of the Holy Family, which adorned the queen's private chapel. Deeply moved, His Majesty dispatched Lebel, the royal pimp, who discovered the thirteen-year-old Louisa living in a Paris attic with her large Irish immigrant family. The frigid Madame de Pompadour was in need of someone to distract the randy king, and this shoemaker's daughter fit the bill. Louise was installed in her own little cottage in Versailles, and for a while threatened to replace Pompadour as the official royal mistress. She bore Louis two children (and had, as well, a third child with Pompadour's husband). Then Louisa spoiled it all, by getting nosy. When she asked Louis if he still had sex with "the old lady," i.e., Pompadour, the enraged monarch threw her out of the palace (with a large dowry) and replaced her with one of her younger sisters.

🏴 **"Battle Annie" Walsh** (mid-nineteenth century) A green-eyed, redhaired Orangewoman, she was the scourge of Hell's Kitchen as leader of the thirty-member Battle Row Ladies Social and Athletic Club. From her headquarters, the back room of a saloon on Fortieth Street and Tenth Avenue, Annie directed her Amazon forces—who she rented out to raise hell on both sides of labor disputes.

🏴 **Lady Jane Francesca Elgee Wilde** (1826–96) She signed her verses and essays "Speranza of the Nation." Her writings were not only vehemently nationalistic but also concerned with the state of poverty in Ireland on the eve of the Great Famine. Her book of Irish history contains a comprehensive study of Celtic traditions and healing herbs, as well as her own eccentric opinions, e.g., that the ancient Egyptian lament "Hi-loo-loo!" was derived from the old Irish wail "Ul-lu-lu!" She married the surgeon oculist to the queen in Ireland, Sir William Wilde, and in her later years moved to London to be closer to her now-famous son, Oscar. During Oscar's trial, when he had a chance to flee England, Speranza convinced him that it was his duty as an "Irish gentleman" to stay, adding, "If you go, I will never speak to you again." A few days after she died, she appeared to her son in his cell at Reading Gaol, dressed in her hat and cloak. During her brief visit, Speranza declined Oscar's offer of a chair.

Appendix I
The Lost Irish Tribes of the South

"The lost Irish tribes of the South are not lost..."
—Irwin S. Cobb, 1931

Touring Dixie recently, the Irish musicians known as the Chieftains feigned astonishment upon discovering how much of Dixie's own country music was derived from traditional Irish tunes.

Although some of its demagogues (e.g., Senators Tom Heflin of Alabama and Ben Tillman of South Carolina) have from time to time proclaimed the white American South to be "100-percent Anglo-Saxon," the fact is that the "British" settlers who colonized the region came, for the most part, from Ireland (North and South), Scotland (Highlands and Lowlands), and Wales. "Almost 75% of the colonial South's population was composed of these 'Celtic' elements," attests the *Encyclopedia of Southern Culture.*

In the eighteenth century, so many new Irish immigrants trekked south that the wagon trail from Philadelphia through Shenandoah to North Carolina was called "the Irish Road." By 1776, over 25 percent of the population of the American South was Irish. They founded towns called Dublin in Georgia, Maryland, Mississippi, North Carolina, Texas, and Virginia.

Even the antebellum "Southern Gentry" (as readers of *Gone with the Wind* need not be reminded) were often of Irish descent. The Hibernian Society of Charleston, South Carolina, was founded in 1798. Historian W. J. Cash began his classic study *The Mind of the South* with "a concrete example of the ruling class...a stout young Irishman [who] brought his bride into the Carolina up-country about 1800." This industrious Irish frontiersman, Cash tells us, in time became a slaveholding cotton baron and patriarch, who was hailed in his 1854 obituary as "a Gentleman... a noble specimen of chivalry at its best."

Novelist John Pendleton Kennedy of Maryland contributed to the "moonlight and magnolias" myth of the Old South, and journalist George Fitzhugh was a staunch advocate of its peculiar economic base—slavery. Fiery secessionist spokesman John C. Calhoun of South Carolina was the son of Pat Calhoun, born in Donegal; his nemesis, Andrew Jackson of South Carolina, was the son of immigrants from Carrickfergus, County Antrim.

The words of the Confederate anthem "The Bonnie Blue Flag" were set to the old Irish tune "The Jaunting Car." While Bishop Patrick Lynch of Charleston toured Europe promoting Dixie's cause, the 24th Georgia, commanded by Robert McMillan from Antrim, mowed down the Union's Irish Brigade at Fredericksburg.

Confederate forces included the Charleston, South Carolina, Irish Volunteers, Alabama's 6th Montgomery Guards, known as Irish Company C and commanded by Major General Robert Emmet Rodes, and the Jefferson Davis Guards of Texas, who won the Battle of Sabine Pass, commanded by Lieutenant Dick Dowling of Galway.

General Sam McGowan of South Carolina assisted in the taking of Fort Sumter. One of Lee's best officers, General Patrick Cleburne, "the Stonewall Jackson of the West," was born in Cork. Patrick Moore of the Virginia Volunteers rose to the rank of brigadier general. The victorious Confederate forces in the Battle of Olustee, Florida, were commanded by Irish-born General Joe Finnegan. General Edward O'Neal, later governor of Alabama, commanded a division at Gettysburg.

The South even fielded two infantry regiments composed of immigrant Irish Catholics, who carried a green flag into battle: the 10th Tennessee, known as the "Rebel Sons of Erin," Colonel Randy McGavock commanding, and the 6th Louisiana "Irish Brigade," for whom, in 1861, this song was published in the *New Orleans True Delta*:

The Irish green shall again be seen
As our Irish fathers bore it
A burning wind from the south behind
And the Yankee route before it!

"Southerners lost the war because they were too Celtic and their opponents were too English," conclude historians McWhiney and Jamison in their study of tactics, *Attack and Die*.

Once the Cause was lost, Father Abram Joseph Ryan, chaplain-poet of the Confederacy, wrote (and generations were obliged to recite) "The Sword of Robert E. Lee."

Journalist John "Irish" Mitchel, who fled Ireland after taking part in the failed revolt of 1848, edited a pro-Confederate newspaper in Richmond, Virginia, and after Lee's surrender was briefly imprisoned with Confederate president Jefferson Davis—whose wife, Varina Howell, was the daughter of another Irish rebel-in-exile.

The post-Reconstruction "New South" was the brain child of an *Atlanta Constitution* editor named William W. Grady. It was vigorously promoted by a pair of congressmen named James Phelan and Darrah "Pig Iron" Kelley.

And the modern South has been explained—or exposed—to the world by Irish-American authors Pat Conroy, Cormac McCarthy, Carson McCullers, Flannery O'Connor, and John Kennedy Toole.

Sad to relate, the Irish of the South have not always been in the forefront of progressive racial politics: the strapping figure of that broth of a boyo, Birmingham, Alabama, sheriff "Bull" Connor, springs to mind.

The Lace-Curtain Irish of the South need only continue to ape the traditions of their betters—the Gentry—back home: erecting stately mansions, riding to hounds, and alternately patronizing and abusing the servants.

In Dixie, the Shanty Irish are variously known as Good Old Boys and Po' White Trash. Their lifestyle is a continuous tribute to their ancient Hibernian origins—a cycle of feuds, jigs, and moonshine. (See *Cracker Culture: Celtic Ways in the Old South* by Grady McWhiney.)

Appendix II
O'Canada

"The freest country left to Irishmen on the face of the earth."
—Thomas D'Arcy McGee, 1867

Now that their wealthy (if slightly ostentatious) American cousins are all reveling in their rediscovered Irishness, it won't be long until the average Canadian (and there is no other kind) sets out in search of his or her Celtic heritage.

The Multicultural Programme of Canada's federal government won't be much help. It has issued publications on the contributions to the nation of the Chinese, Germans, Jews, Poles, Portuguese, Scots, Ukrainians, and West Indians. Nothing, so far, about the Irish, although in the last census before asking questions about ethnic origins was eschewed—that is, in 1961—10 percent of Canadians claimed to be of Irish descent.

We may assume, moreover, that the true number of Irish Canadians is considerably larger, because in Canada it is widely (and erroneously) believed that a) Irish = Catholic, and b) Irish = descendant of post-1845 famine immigrants.

In fact, before the potato blight—between 1824 and 1845—almost half a million souls (the vast majority of them Anglicans and Presbyterians) emigrated from Ireland to British North America. (It may be assumed that some of them immediately proceeded, with dubious legality, across the border to the USA.)

But the original Irish Canadians were Catholics, crewmen serving (involuntarily) with British cod-fishing fleets. Around 1675, they began to spend the winter—that is, to "settle"—in Newfoundland. Today, one third of all Newfies are of Irish descent—and look and sound it.

In 1761, Protestant farmers were imported from Ulster to occupy the expropriated farms of the exiled Acadians. By the end of the eighteenth century, Irish immigrants, both Protestant and Catholic, to the Maritimes were so numerous that both the provinces now called New Brunswick and Nova Scotia were once known as New Ireland.

The first Irish in New France/Lower Canada/Quebec were mercenaries, "Wild Geese" serving there in the French army's Irish brigades. In 1760, they defeated the British at the battle of Carrillon, but returned to Quebec City too late to aid General Montcalm in its defense. After the conquest, these Irish soldiers were assimilated into the Habitant community. Over the years, O'Sullivans became Sylvains, Leahys became De La Hayes, and O'Reillys became Riels. Thus, a century later, Louis Riel, the leader of the 1885 Red River Rebellion in Manitoba, felt entitled to emblazon his battle flag with both a fleur-de-lys and a shamrock. Riel's war with Canada began with his execution of an Ontario Orangeman, Thomas Scott.

The majority of Orangemen were, and are, Irishmen—Protestant ones, bound by an oath of loyalty to the British crown. The Grand Orange Lodge of British America was founded in Brockville, Ontario—then Upper Canada—in 1830; by 1860, the order claimed (with, perhaps, some exaggeration) 100,000 Canadian members.

Ontario—now the nation's most populous and prosperous province—was settled by Irish immigrants. Many, but not all, were Protestants. Many, but not all, came from Ulster. Some were among the United Empire Loyalists who fled to Canada from the rebellious United States in 1776. Some were Protestant Irish of the Ascendancy class, who fled to Canada from rebellious Ireland in 1798. Some were soldiers discharged from the British Army after the War of 1812, to whom the crown offered grants of land along the Ottawa River. In 1818 alone, 4,599 Irish men, women, and children embarked from Cork to Canada. In 1823, Peter Robinson induced five hundred Irish Catholics to settle in the area now known—in his honor—as Peterborough. By 1867, fully two thirds of Ontarians were of Irish birth or descent, because another 150,000 Irish natives had arrived—the survivors of the plague-infested "coffin ships" in which they crossed the Atlantic.

In Ireland, in the years of the Great Hunger, a million paupers died. Another million emigrated—half of them to Canada—because they were evicted tenant farmers, whose landlords sometimes subsidized their fare, and passage to the British colony was far cheaper than a ticket to Boston or New York.

Tens of thousands of them—perhaps one in five—never made it. They perished of typhus or cholera, en route or in quarantine. In the year known as Black '47, 22,000 Irish would-be immigrants to Canada—men, women, and children—died: 5,000 at sea, 2,000 at St. John, New Brunswick, 8,000 at Quebec, 7, 000 at Montreal.

Unlike the farming, landholding Protestant Irish who had preceded them, these impoverished Catholic newcomers were, perforce, urban, occupying tenements in the Paddytowns and Mick Alleys of the cities at which they had disembarked. (In 1866, there were fifty thousand Irish in Montreal.)

Together, the Orange and the Green were—or might have been—a force to be reckoned with, as when, in 1890, a parliamentary bill was introduced by Senator Thomas McInnes of Nova Scotia, proposing to make Gaelic Canada's third official language. Together, he pointed out, the Scots and Irish numbered 1,657,000—making Celts the nation's largest single ethnic group.

As we pursue Canadian Celticity, the question before us is: *What happened to all those Micks?* One answer, at least, is "The Fenians."

In 1866, British North America was invaded by an army whose leaders intended to establish an Irish government-in-exile there. This Fenian force (the first in history to style itself an "Irish Republican Army") had the tacit—and "deniable"—approval of U.S. president Andrew Johnson.

By the last day of May, more than 10,000 Fenians (including 500 Mohawk Indians and 100 black Union Army veterans) had massed along the border. On June 1, led by Colonel John O'Neill (born in County Monaghan, now resident of Nashville, Tennessee), 1,200 troops crossed the border and advanced on Fort Erie, defeating the Canadian militia in a pitched battle at Rideway. But for reasons of their own, 8,000 other Fenian troops remained behind in Buffalo, whither, after five days of losing skirmishes in Canada, O'Neill and his troops were obliged to retreat.

On June 5, Brigadier Samuel S. Spear led 2,000 Fenians into French Canada from St. Alban's, Vermont, with a similar lack of success.

Historians agree that the uniting and founding of Canada—Confederation, 1876—was one consequence of these Fenian raids. But surely another result is that a million embarrassed Canadian Irish opted to fade into the Anglo-Saxon wallpaper for a century or so.

About the Authors

SEAN KELLY is umpteenth-generation Canadian-Irish. He left teaching to edit the *National Lampoon*. He writes for children's television (*Noddy and Friends*) and is co-author of several books, including *Saints Preserve Us!*, *Who in Hell...*, and *Boom Baby Moon*.

ROSEMARY ROGERS is the co-author of *Saints Preserve Us!*, *Who in Hell...*, and *Boomer Babes*. Her mother was born in Emyvale, County Monaghan, and her father was born in Drumlish, County Longford.